AmoS

the churchmouse

many blessings to
you from the
church pew underworld —
amos
a.ka. —
Gary Re

Amos

the churchmouse

a view from under the pew

Gary Mitchell

Illustrated by Ron Wheeler

Pleasant Word
A Division of WINEPRESS PUBLISHING

Pleasant Word (a division of WinePress Publishing, PO Box 428, Enumclaw, WA 98022) functions only as book publisher. As such, the ultimate design, content, editorial accuracy, and views expressed or implied in this work are those of the author.

Unless otherwise noted, all Scriptures are taken from the King James Version of the Bible.

Scripture references marked NASB are taken from the New American Standard Bible, © 1960, 1963, 1968, 1971, 1972, 1973, 1975, 1977 by The Lockman Foundation. Used by permission.

ISBN 13: 978-1-4141-1175-9
ISBN 10: 1-4141-1175-4
Library of Congress Catalog Card Number: 2008900392

To Judy with love
To Mara, Aubrey & Thomas with joy
To Mom and Dad with deep gratitude
But above all—to God be the glory

Contents

Acknowledgments

The author is indebted to *Plains Faith* and *Voices* magazines for permission to reprint these columns.

And the author gratefully acknowledges that many of these columns were previously published in the *Clovis News Journal.*

The Coming of Amos

While I was pastor of a small church in a medium-sized community, an unusual phenomenon occurred in my life, which I am discovering is difficult to put into words. Still, I thought perhaps a number of readers might find some curious amusement in it. That strange phenomenon concerns the coming of a small, gray churchmouse, now transplanted to our fair community, who...uh...writes free verse poetry.

I know what you're thinking: *Sure, uh-huh. Another loony preacher who cracked under the strain—too many sermons, late-night counseling sessions, and all that sort of thing.*

I realize how it must sound, and although I may have been eating more cheese lately, I haven't retrieved my Mickey Mouse ears out of the old trunk—yet.

Here, then, are the facts surrounding the strange incident involving Amos. If after you read this explanation you have some question about its authenticity, Amos tells me he's prepared to offer as evidence his mother's family Bible (bound in traditional cheesecloth), which traces his lineage back to that famous, American, primitive artist, Grandma Mouses.

Our relationship goes back to my pre-college days when I was editor of our church's youth newsletter (a prestigious and much sought-after position: "Here, you take it"…"No, you take it"). Late one night, I walked into the church's newsletter office, which consisted of an old, moldy coffee cup and a couple of old computers and a printer placed strategically between a stack of paper and a wastebasket. I was about to finish the next issue's layout when I heard some strange pecking noises coming from an old computer in the corner cubicle. I cautiously tiptoed to it and peeked into the cubicle. An unusual sight confronted me.

The old word processor had been left on, and a small, gray mouse (in an awkward imitation of Don Marquis's famous poetic cockroach, Archy) was doggedly catapulting himself from one letter to another on the computer keyboard. I started to chase it away, thinking it was just another poor creature who had unfortunately taken a sip from the office coffeepot.

But the little fellow intrigued me, and I sat down to watch. He worked slowly, having to backspace quite often since it seemed the more he threw himself at the keyboard, the worse his aim got. Obviously, he couldn't type and work the capital shift at the same time. He shunned the punctuation keys (except for the dash, for some odd reason) as if they were quicksand bogs.

I was on the verge of deciding he was some scientist's frustrated experimental mouse, and the victim of extreme psychological-maze-pattern fatigue, when his occasional tappings stopped. I peeped over the computer terminal just before he fell, exhausted. He lay in a collapsed heap in the middle of the space bar.

The next morning, much to my surprise, I found a poem typed in a legible manner on the computer screen. We printed it, and that was the beginning of our relationship.

Amos was a simple, poetic churchmouse back then, trading his narrative poetry for stale doughnut crumbs and spilled coffee or Kool-Aid (a royal bounty compared to the dried sermons and stuffy songbook covers he was used to choking down). However, as the months passed by, Amos began to feel that his diet (both physical and spiritual) lacked substance.

So when I offered him the chance to go to college with me, I think he fairly jumped at it (but I'm not sure since he doesn't jump very high anyway). In college, he learned to express himself freely and positively—almost to extremes. In seminary, he felt a little stifled, but he learned to appreciate some of those dry sermons over which he once frowned.

Now back home in a local church, next to a satellite campus of Wayland Baptist University, he has made new friends and resumed what he calls his calling: "Doing hack poetry for the enlightenment of the church pew underworld." (He still calls me "boss," harking back to the days when I was his editor for the church youth newsletter.)

Following is what he wrote in his debut column.

the coming of amos

i am neither a symbol of a
religio-political party
nor am i an escapee from a
research laboratory

as you so kindly
consider me to be
coming here as i do
i have no axe to grind
boss
only whiskers
to brush and a tail
to look after

i come to share
the experience
of under-the-church-pew
relationships
mouse to mouse
mouse to bugs
and other
minority groups
mouse to choir
mouse to preacher
but mostly
the mouse to jesus one

but don t get me wrong
boss
i am neither a crusader
sword in hand out to do
battle with the religions
of the world
nor a gloriously converted
brawling street rat

The Coming of Amos

nor am i an angelic
manifestation wrapped
in mouseskin
coming here as i do

i come to flee
the glazed-over
stale sermonic doughnuts
and the flashy hardcover
sourdough songbooks
of mediocre christianity
so popular in some
churches these days
which wouldn t be
so bad
boss
but they re
nearly always substituted
for the bread of life
and the joyful noise

i come to seek
the real bread of life
and to taste the wine
of a poured-out soul
in service to one s
fellow animalkind
that is if you don t
have any stale doughnuts
or sourdough songbooks

to discourage me
boss

you may say what does
a little gray mouse
know about life
or about anything
listen
boss
life ain t easy under a
cushionless church pew
in fact
clara centipede
contends that more
careless casualties
occur in church
than anywhere else
in the world
i don t know about
that
boss
but clara says it
with so much authority
and conviction
and stamps all thirty-two
of her feet
so that nobody argues
with her
at any rate
no dallas freeway

The Coming of Amos

can match a church aisle
at high noon

but most of all
i come to write
to express the freedom
of my soul
and where better
to do that than
for a church newsletter
question mark here
boss

i come to write because
like archy the cockroach
i feel expression
is the need
of my soul
but unlike archy
that expression
is not of me
but of christ in me
and after all
boss
isn t it
in him that every living
creature finds expression—
even mice and little men

the other day
tommy tarantula found

his expression
boss
he painted
sally spider s web black
last night
sally got herself
tangled up
in the dark

i sympathize with her
boss
because like her
the rest of my world
and i
were tangled up in the dark too
but that was before
i encountered the light
of the world
and learned from him
how to walk in light

and even though i realize
darkness has no power
in the face
of shining light
it entices me
and i cover myself
in black
and go back for a visit
but only to discover
what i already knew before—

The Coming of Amos

how messy it was
to be tangled up
in the dark
in the first place

amos

p s—if you leave the computer
turned on
i will write again
next time—
that is if i can
find a way
to neutralize your coffee
boss
i licked some yesterday
and it made
my tail kinky

Amos Launches
a Crusade

Amos hasn't been satisfied with sharing rutty lectures and routine meetings with other mousey Christians—despite how inspiring Pastor Leroy Beetle's prayers and sermons sometimes are. In a cover letter to his column, he cited some of his complaints.

i am tired
tired of sad meetings
that inspire me
for five minutes
before i go home to bed

i am fed up
with the grape juice and crackers
of meaningless communions

the old broken-down church
in the far corner
has suddenly aged
and grown stiff and cold
rigid and brittle—
inflexible to the times

With such dissatisfaction, he reversed and launched his own campaign to conquer the world for Christianity.

amos launches a crusade

the spirit of the crusader
rages within me
boss
i am setting up
my personal size
ivory soap box
and am dragging out
my salvation army trumpet—
yesterday we marched against
the communal cockroaches
next week
we conquer
the humanistic humbugs

though we blitzed
those dreaded red cockroaches
with the two-edged sword
boss
they still resist
and lack the faith
in fact
some carry signs
saying atheism forever—
down with prayer—

may your faith
die in the night
and your children
grow up to be little red
card-carrying communal cockroaches

martyrs are common
stanley spider died yesterday
in the clutches of an atheistic
brillo soap pad
in a valiant blitz
to christianize
a cockroach-infested sink
saddened we buried stanley
in the garbage disposal
with full military honors
and returned home
to be inspired
by leroy beetle

sometimes
boss
the spirit
of the crusader
speaks louder than
his spears
and often returns
to haunt him
perhaps the most horrific thing
about a rebellious

and warring spirit
is that it s already
a lost cause—
unless it is tempered
by the timeless triumph
of the holy spirit s love

amos

p s—my tail s still kinky
from last week s coffee
boss
i appreciated the offer of
your neutralizer
last night—a little bit
of horseradish
goes a long way
doesn t it—
and even though
it did make the hair
on the back of my tail
stand up
it still wasn t
the antidote needed
to get the kinks out

it s really a problem
the other day
a reporter from
the bugtussle sentinel

came to me
asking for
an exclusive interview
with the world s
smallest gray piglet

Amos Goes to Ohio

Of late, Amos has become obsessed with the thought of missions. One day, he walked across a picture of a starving, orphaned mouse in India, and he claims the innocent little fellow's gaunt face and emaciated whiskers haunted him every night until he decided to do something about it.

For one thing, he replaced all of his "Cheeses of the World" posters (which lined the walls of his cozy matchbox home) with pictures of gaunt, starving animals from all over the world.

In addition, he has become a regular contributor to the Worldwide Three-Blind-Mice Aid to the Disabled Fund, and has started shipping all his old, woolen mittens (which he found once upon a time but thinks they must have belonged to three little kittens) to all the poor Eskimo mice in Alaska.

He even doubled his donation to the Lottie Mouse Christmas Offering, but he still felt that he should be more personally involved in the missions effort. When the opportunity opened for him to go with a mission team to Ohio, his eagerness to go bubbled over into one of his columns.

amos goes to ohio

the lord has told me
to meet him in ohio
boss
that s where he said
the harvest will be

at first i was so excited
boss
i nearly forgot to pack my bible
and then i was so ashamed
of my forgetfulness
that i debated
whether i ought
to take me or not

it didn t take the devil long
to pick up the message
on his new-fangled intercom system
and when he approached me
he wasn t dressed
in anything so recognizable
as a fire-engine red
serpent s suit

wrapped in a kindly old
saint s shawl he offered me
a green stomach that
trembled all the time

he came to me again
in explorer s boots
and a knapsack
brandishing for me
a heart inflated with
lusty adventure

retreating then
to the saintly shawl
he came to me
a third time
looking more like
a gangster s moll
than a kindly old saint—
and he tommy-gunned me down
with my inadequacies

while i was lying in a heap there
at the bottom of the valley road
jesus passed by
and gave me enough strength
to look to him
and in looking to him
i was lifted up
and filled to balloon-size
with his spirit—
there was a big hole
in my balloon
and his spirit kept flowing out
but i never deflated

and my balloon
is flying me
to ohio
boss
but sometimes
my tail hangs down
and drags the ground
the devil steps on it
once in a while
but one of these days
he ll get a hot foot
for what he s been doing

amos

Willifred's Rocket Launchings

willifred s rocket launchings

one day last month
the lord told willifred the white rat—
you remember willifred
boss
he was a mad scientist s
experimental mouse
before his conversion—
to launch three match-rockets
and to call them
experience one two and three
and even though he didn t understand
it all he started doing it anyway

first of all willifred collected
three brillo soap pads
for launch pads
and painted them
red white and blue
like he thought nasa would do
but he used more white than red and blue
partly because it was the lord s work
and his work
ought to be characterized by purity

but mainly because the white
was on special at sara spider s
underground discount house

by the time willifred had erected
his three match-rockets
on the brillo launch pads
the mouse media had the story
and were on the scene
publicity lifted willifred
to the height of his ego—
he was in the national news
he was televised with
pioneer space experts
he was interviewed for his opinion
on everything from the morals
of trap-door spiders to whether
the mouse world can survive
the cheese freeze—and then the
day came for the first launch

it was an unspoiled success
boss
and the congratulations sent
his head spinning
but he said he was careful
to thank the lord for it all
and he felt certain
he was in the lord s will

the launch of experience two came
and went without much fanfare
oh there were a few minor
newspapers and radio stations
on hand for it but nobody
really cared about it all
willifred was all sad
and dejected and disappointed
it was all so blah
boss

willifred then decided
to postpone the third shot
not so much to wait on the lord
but more to build up publicity
and get the media excited again—
he sponsored luncheons
he held contests
he invited space experts
to speak about the importance of
the work—and finally they were
ready for the shot of experience three
even though willifred had had a
bad nightmare about it the
night before

the match-rocket was lit
and everyone gasped
as it started up
but then for no apparent reason

it toppled over on its side
and burned up

willifred was crushed
boss
the end of the world
was upon him
he kept asking
where is the lord
and why did it happen
and where is the cheese
gonna come from now
and the world is cruel and unkind—
defeat seemed sure
boss
but all the lord wanted
to teach willifred was not
to blow his mind on life s
circumstantial experiences

amos

Amos on Love

Due to an unfortunate circumstance beyond almost anyone's control, it has been rather difficult trying to make Amos keep up with his writing. Normally, he's eager to write and grateful for the opportunity to do it.

But there is nothing "normal" about his behavior now. He just sits on the space bar and stares into space. It appears that he's fallen in love (although he prefers to say that he "grew in love"—and it does seem to have a more natural ring to it) with the little girl mouse next door.

As his love grew, our paper supply dwindled proportionately. He wrapped her flowers with and wrote her songs and poems on our church's copier paper, tissues, toilet paper, and kitchen napkins. She is about all he thinks of anymore, so he presents this column.

amos on love

boss my head is spinning—
i suppose you found out
about jenny the mouse
next door
i noticed the little freeway
you built from my matchbox

to hers
and the two signs at each end
that read sourly
mouse-to-mouse communication

maybe i didn t appreciate it
at the time
boss
but that phrase
says quite a lot

after all
what is love but a deeper communication—
a communication that is
more than just
the sharing of words and thoughts
but the sharing of ourselves

i feel a feeling
composed of many feelings
none of which resemble
heartburn or acid indigestion
as you so profoundly suggested
yesterday
and my love wasn t at all affected
by your alka-seltzer

my love ripples
and flows within me
its swells lash
into the boat-filled bays
of my consciousness
affecting even the dirt beaches
of my external world—
jenny s love for christ
and for me
has deepened my own awareness
and love for christ
in fact
it has made my life
an amplifier of his love
everywhere

for when two in love
love jesus more
jesus loves through the two
deeper than either loved before

looking at this now
boss
i think a mouse s efforts
would be in vain
and have no purpose
if he knows no experience
of jesus love—
his would be the empty life

amos

p s—boss
about the paper supply
i don t know what
you ve been doing with it all
but we re running low on typing paper
so when you order the next ream
get the kind with
the yellow and blue flowers
and ducks all over it
jenny likes the flowers
i like the ducks

The Death of Prayer Virgil, Part One

Of late, tragedy has struck the church pew underworld. It is an event that forebodes serious implications for future prayer meetings.

the death of prayer virgil

there is a sadness here
we all feel
boss
the death of prayer virgil
you remember him
the praying mantis
who used to visit us
each Wednesday evening
he died of loneliness
we think
no one knows for sure
we weren t around
when it happened

some of us still mourn his passing
at times we gather together
just to replay his funeral

and other times
it s almost like he was here

the other day
brownie beagle came by
while sammy salamander and i
were speculating on the untimely
end of poor prayer virgil
it s so sad
sammy was saying
he wanted so much to be
the spirit of the place
yes that s so
brownie echoed
you could even see
the look of peace
on his face

but now he s gone
we re left alone
no more quiet
only fights to the end
then over again
oops ran out of paper
boss
will continue my
tale of woe next time

amos

p s—and please don t put
that silly blue stationery
with the little yellow duckies
in your computer anymore
somehow it just doesn t seem
to fit the format

The Death of Prayer Virgil, Part Two

Amos, the transplanted, poetic churchmouse, continued his sad tale about the death of Prayer Virgil, the lovable praying mantis who used to visit the church pew underworld each Wednesday evening.

At last count, Amos and several friends were gathered around the family Bible in the prayer room, discussing poor Prayer Virgil's unfortunate demise, when Bertie Woeworm crawled from the hall into the room, sobbing.

the death of prayer virgil
part two

he was killed
bertie woeworm was crying
as he crawled along in the hall
murdered by indifference
overcome by negligence
pushed aside
by overzealous preachers
sat upon
by careless committees
trampled over
by a world-hungry congregation
we re guilty everyone

bertie came crying
on his way
it s so sad
sammy continued to say

what s so sad
why all the gloom and doom
louie the songdog sang
as he padded by
what s happened to your glad
have you not heard
he smiled and said
there s a rumor in the city
a murmur in the country
they say prayer virgil is not dead
he s alive
but not so well
he s weak and faint
but dead he ain t

fantastic quotation marks and
an exclamation point here
boss
brownie beagle barked
how about that
sammy salamander wiggled
even bertie woeworm
managed a grin

i wouldn t have believed it
boss

but a fellow with a changed heart
and a happy song
can reshape the world

amos

p s—by the way
boss
your stationery with
the molded green cheese
was in very poor taste
i d rather have the little duckies

The Grasshopper's Dilemma

the grasshopper s dilemma

once upon a time
boss
a young smart-alecky
grasshopper bounded
across the path of a
little elderly gray-feathered
lady owl named olivia

god bless you
young man
says olivia
in her characteristic
good-natured manner

what do you mean
god bless you
says greg
the smart-alecky bugaboo
i don t believe in god
and neither should you
there s no such being
either here
or beyond the blue

why my dear
how can you say that
says olivia
without a flap
for such a young fellow
you re as sarcastic as a cat

i once believed
there was a god
says greg
without a nod
but now
thanks to my studies
in philosophy and math
i m convinced there is
no god of love or wrath
i threw him out
with the bath
to me he s an empty word
the thought of him is
simply absurd

well says she
i haven t studied such things
so studiously
but since you ve done so
maybe you can let me know
from whence came that
chicken egg so white
as snow

The Grasshopper's Dilemma

certainly i can
says he with a grin
of course
it comes from a hen

and from where then comes
that feisty little hen
asked olivia
a second time again

why from an egg
says the bored grasshopper
named greg

very gently
sweet olivia inquired then
which existed first the egg or the hen—
which one was prior my friend

the hen of course
says greg
this is such
a silly discourse

bear with me a bit
i m just trying to learn
says olivia
with a slight turn
then a hen must have existed
without coming from an egg

is that right
young studious greg

well no says he
somewhat thoughtfully
i should have said
the egg was first—
it took priority

then i suppose you mean
says olivia
with a hint of a gleam
that one lone egg
came to be without a hen
for its mommy
at once exasperated
the young grasshopper hesitated
well you see
says he
it must be—
well it had to be—
the hen came first
and had priority

very well
says she
rather knowingly
now let me see
if i understand—
without an egg to begin
who made that first hen

from which has descended
all other succeeding
eggs and hens

by now young greg s
little grasshopper face
was red with anger
and disgrace
what do you mean by this

why simply this—
that he who created the first egg
or hen
is he who created the world
and made it spin
you can t explain the start
of an egg or a hen
without god s hand
but you want me to believe
that you can expand
on how the world came to be
without god or his ingenuity

amos

Amos and
The Prodigal Flea

Amos, the self-proclaimed churchmouse poet laureate, has become distressed in recent days about reports he has been reading in the *Bugtussle Sentinel* concerning the plight of youth in the church pew underworld.

It seems there is an alarming increase in the statistics of young bugs drinking sewer water, snorting rat poison, committing suicide by jumping into toilet bowls (labeled by the mouse media as "commodal suicide"), and smoking discarded broomstick bristles.

The problem has reached epidemic proportions in the underworld society. And to complicate the matter more, young bugs, fleas, ticks, roaches, and rats—from all strata of society—are running away in large numbers. In fact, "Runaway Bug and Rodent Syndrome" (RBRS) is fast becoming the gravest psycho-social problem in the history of the church pew underworld. Panel discussions, talk shows, and investigative reports have flooded the mouse media.

Amos's own awareness of the problem was heightened by an encounter with a runaway flea.

amos and the prodigal flea

boss
i ran into despair yesterday

freddie flea was lying
in a heap
next to the garbage can

looky here
says he to me
the symbol of my life
he pointed with a shaky hand
to the rusty can

i could write a book
on how to snarf and hook
from under the pan

sounds bad
says i
what do you mean
everything says he

Amos and The Prodigal Flea

life is dead
he said
when a bug is head
strong to go on the road—
a rosebed it ain t
he said
and dropped his head

but why
says i to the runaway
did you fly away
in the first place

he looks at me
sorta strangely
and says what s your case
his eyes searched my face
are you a bug-chiatrist
he asked
and shook his fist
no says i
just an ordinary guy

then i ll tell you
says he
i ran away for me
to live and to be free
but you said
i said
i know what i said
he said

life on the street is death
there s no place for a breath
of fresh air anywhere

then why not come upstairs
says i
where there s cool air
and fair skies

how can that be
says he

it s a matter of
redirecting your focus
says i
no hocus-pocus
if ya want to find real life
look to the creator of life
only he can abolish strife

but
he says to me
how—can i find it even now

sure
i chortled joyously
look you wanted to live free
to live for yourself and fly
so ya lunged at life and died
the more you grabbed
the less you had

Amos and The Prodigal Flea

that s right
he said
it s like a blight

here s why
says i
if ya wanna live
ya gotta die

it sounds like a lie
to me
says he

but the more you cling
more death it ll bring
said i in reply
ya gotta choose
to lose your life
to christ
if ya wanna win
this battle over sin
and strife

but to give up my life
says he
it s the only way to victory
says i
then you can fly
move up on high
climb into the upstairs lane
live life on a higher plane

but
says he
to die to self
and put my dreams on a shelf—
i don t know
says he
maybe—just maybe—
to trade away my misery
for life peace and victory
maybe that s for me

amos

p s—oh by the way
boss
your book on how to
win friends and influence
prodigal fleas was of
no help to me—for one thing
the advice to help them
find a bigger dog
has turned the entire
canine community
against me—as if cats
weren t enough—
and your second bit
of advice to buy them
all a large scoop of
ice cream proved
equally disastrous—
tell me what am i

supposed to do with
an ice cream cone
full of frozen fleas
question mark

Life in a Matchbox

life in a matchbox
solomon s proverbs paraphrased

boss
i may have mentioned this
once before
but life ain t easy
under a cushionless church pew

a wise mouse lays up knowledge
as a squirrel stores up nuts—
except knowledge lasts longer—
especially if you eat as much
as stanley squirrel does

he who gathers in the summer
is a wise mouse
but he who hops around
and parties with the grasshoppers
causes shame for
his momma and poppa mouse

a gossipy ladybug
reveals secrets and
scatters pain but a

faithful closed-mouthed
friend keeps harmony in
the church pew underworld

he who withholds
his cheese
the other mice shall curse
but blessing shall be
upon the head of him
who generously shares

as a golden ring
in a pig s snout
so is a lovely ladybug
with rude manners
or a foul mouth

he who creates misery
within his own little
matchbox will inherit
the wind—and probably
a few flames as well

just as doing what s
right tendeth to life
so he who pursues evil
will pursue it to his
own death

young mouse
walk not in the ways

of the wild rat
or the heathen alley cat
for their feet run to
evil to maim the young
and old and to steal and
spoil the food they find
they plot and scheme
and lay snares for
others but instead find
themselves ensnared in
their own traps

the young mouse who chooses
to live right shall receive
wisdom and long life
but the mouse who chooses
wickedness and foolish living
will one day have to pay
for traveling the wrong way

never yell at a neighbor mouse
when you re eating cheese
or crackers

never chase your tail—
one of four things almost
always happens
either you
exhaust yourself
and fall flat on your nose
or you get dizzy

and fall flat on your nose
or you stumble and
fall flat on your nose
or even if you actually
catch your tail
what then
question mark here
boss

never get mad and
kick the cheese in a
mouse trap

a spring-loaded
mouse trap is like
a fifty-ton freight train—
you can t outrun
either of them

peace and long life
shall follow
the mouse who
sips the milk of kindness
shuns the wine of bitterness
walks the way of love
shares the bread and
cheese of life and
stops often at the
well of forgiveness

amos

The Saga of Willie Badmouth

the saga of willie badmouth

boss
you remember willie
the woolie worm well that s
what we used to call him

but willie has been
progressively developing
his vocabulary building in
highly regressive ways

in other words
boss
he cusses up a storm

his bawdy elocutions spew
forth like old faithful s geyser
his nasty epitaphs
have horrified most church
pew underworld folks
his verbal diatribes have stunted
the growth of most larvae
and all the cute little tadpoles
in the pond not to mention

causing all the ladybugs to
turn varying shades of red

at first the young cockroaches
and termite toughies thought it
was pretty cool but then even
they got sick of it and went
back to their home looting
and building destruction duties

some of the church deacon
bugs fireflies and the hoppy
toads tried to persuade him
to tone down the vernacular
but he wouldn t listen
it was like his brain was missing
he kept yelling and cursing all
the way down the track-ular

the woeworms complained
that willie badmouth—or the
cursing caterpillar of the south—
his new monikers now boss—
was too negative
even for them
he was always
spreading rumors and griping
about his fellow animalkind

it was a minor crisis in the
church pew underworld

finally when willie noticed
that no one wanted to hang
around with him anymore
his loneliness drove him
straight to prayer virgil
the praying mantis s door

willie appeared to be
truly repentant
boss
he wept
woolie tears and confessed
his ungodly slander and
painful nameslaying

prayer virgil s only words
of healing and comfort were
my son to die to your selfish
ways is the best and only gain

you must forsake those
hellish curses and phrases
speak only truth in love and
cease to cause any pain

but i don t know how to stop
in time i can t control this
tongue of mine

only by dying to yourself and
letting jesus live in you

can you break free of your
wordy prison of pain

enjoy life and a whole
vocabulary anew—you can
break into a sky of blue—
and have jesus victory and
heaven to gain

and
boss
with those words
of wisdom willie wrapped
himself in a cocoon of
seeming death—only to
burst forth into a
beautiful butterfly of
praise for all the world
to see

amos

Amos on Anger

AMOS ON ANGER

SOMEBODY SABOTAGED
THE COMPUTER
BOSS
IN CASE YOU COULDN T TELL
THEY LEFT THE CAPITAL SHIFT
LOCKED DOWN
AND I M BEATING
MY BRAINS OUT
JUST TRYING TO COMMUNICATE
CAN T YOU DO SOMETHING
BOSS
EVERYTHING I WRITE
HAS A SENSE OF
EMERGENCY ABOUT IT
EVEN A RESTAURANT
MENU PRINTED IN THESE
LARGE UNGODLY LETTERS
WOULD SOUND EITHER
HIGHLY CONTAGIOUS OR
DANGEROUS

THESE GIANT LETTERS
ARE DRIVING ME TO

DISTRACTION
I CAN T
THINK OR CONTEMPLATE
ANYTHING OF ANY
MAJOR SIGNIFICANCE
I FEEL LIKE I M
SCREAMING FOR NO
GOOD REASON LIKE
SOME PREACHERS AND
POLITICIANS I HAVE
KNOWN

I AM ANGRY
WITHOUT A CAUSE

MAD AT A SAPPY
SABOTEUR WHETHER
HE PERPETRATED HIS
CRIME DELIBERATELY
OR ACCIDENTALLY IS
OF NO REAL CONCERN
TO ME I AM JUST
MAD ABOUT IT

MAD AT A MAKESHIFT
MALFUNCTIONING
MISERABLE COMPUTER
THAT COULDN T CARE LESS
WHETHER I M MAD
AT IT OR NOT
ALL IT DOES IS JUST
SIT AND STARE AND
SNEER AT ME IN
LARGE CAPITAL
LETTERS

BUT MOST OF ALL I M
MAD AT ME
MAD BECAUSE I M SO LITTLE
AND UNCOORDINATED
AND THIS COMPUTER
IS SO BIG AND STUBBORN
BOSS
I AM SERIOUSLY
CONSIDERING SIGNING UP

FOR MIGHTY MARVIN S
MUSCLEBOUND MOUSE
COURSE OR HOW TO
BECOME A SEVEN-TO
NINE-POUND RODENT IN
NINETY DAYS OR YOUR
MONEY BACK
IT S ALSO CALLED THE
DON T-BE-AN-
EIGHT-OUNCE-WEAKLING-
BE-THE-BIGGEST-RAT-
ON-YOUR-BLOCK SEMINAR
I REALLY DON T WANT
TO SIGN UP FOR IT
BUT I M ANGRY AND
I M UPSET AND I M MAD
ENOUGH TO EAT
AN OLD STALE SERMON
OR GNAW MY WAY
THROUGH A HARDCOVER
SONGBOOK

LET ME TELL YOU
BOSS
IT S A TERRIBLE
AWFUL FRUSTRATING
THING TO BE MAD
AND NOT REALLY HAVE
ANYTHING TO BE MAD AT
THAT WAS THE STATE OF
MY SOUL WHEN LOUIE

THE SONGDOG PADDED
HAPPILY BY

BE QUIET SAYS I
OR I LL POKE YOU
IN THE EYE

YOU RE TALKING
MIGHTY TOUGH
SAYS HE
FOR SUCH LITTLE
STUFF

I M MAD
SAYS I
AND THAT S NO LIE

THEN TELL ME WHY

I M MAD AT A MACHINE
AT EVERYTHING IN
THE WORLD AND ALL
I M MAD AT
SOMEBODY MYSELF
AND NOBODY AT ALL
I M SO MIXED UP ALL I
WANNA DO IS BAWL

THERE AIN T NO CALL
TO TOSS IN THE BALL

YOU NEED TO GET
RID OF YOUR MAD
AND FORGET ABOUT
YOUR PLIGHT SO SAD
THESE LETTERS
AIN T SO BAD
THERE S NO NEED
TO RUN AND HIDE
YOU RE JUST
TANGLED UP IN PRIDE
NOW WHAT
YOU REALLY NEED TO DO
IS THANK THE LORD
SING HALLELU

YOU RE CRAZY
SAYS I
YOU RE A NICE GUY
BUT I MAY STILL
SPIT IN YOUR EYE

THAT S FINE BY ME
SAYS HE
BUT LISTEN
TO ME PATIENTLY
AND I THINK YOU LL
SEE I M SHOWING YOU
THE WAY TO VICTORY

BUT HOW CAN I SING
AND SHOUT WITH GLEE

WHEN I M FEELING SO
MISERABLY

IT S NOT SO EASY
SAYS HE
BUT YOU
CAN DO IT IF YOU LL
LISTEN TO ME
THE SECRET OF NOT
STAYING ANGRY IS
TO LET GO YOUR PRIDE
AND PRAISE FREELY

BUT WHAT S TO PRAISE
SAYS ME IN LETTERS
AS BIG AS TREES

PLENTY
SAYS HE
JUST THINK HOW GREAT
AND HOW ARTICULATE
THE GOOD NEWS CAN BE
FOR ALL TO SEE
IN LETTERS SO BOLD
AND TALL AS THESE

HE WAS RIGHT
BOSS
I AM ASHAMED
IN LARGE CAPITALS I HAVE
MISUSED MY MISFORTUNE

ABUSED MY ABERRATION
AND TRANSGRESSED ON
MY TRAGEDY

BUT ALL IS NOT LOST
THERE S NO REASON
TO BE SO BLUE
I CAN STILL SAY IN ALL HONESTY
THAT GOD LOVES ME AND YOU

AMOS

Spooky Superstitions

spooky superstitions

weird things have been
happening to me recently
boss
it s like some black cat
has been planning my
things-to-do list

first of all
i didn t want
to get out of bed
especially after
last night s dream
i dreamed of an invasion
of alien black cats
who had a secret sonar system
to ferret out little mice
like me
boss

then i tried to tiptoe
past the custodian
while he was mopping
the kitchen floor

but he dumped water
all over me

while i was shaking myself dry
my tail swished around
and found the nearest
electrical outlet—
and no this is not my new
hairstyle—so what if i look
like a frizzy tennis ball

i had just about decided
to leave the animal kingdom
for a nice cave
in yellowstone park
when georgie the gypsy moth
came flittering by

it s spooky ole halloween
amos
he sang
almost joyfully
what happened to you
my fuzzy friend
you look like the fattest hairy
caterpillar i ve ever seen

thanks a lot
says i
you re an awfully cheerful soul
i thought all gypsy moths

Spooky Superstitions

were a superstitious lot
it looks like it ll be a real
doozy of a halloween

aw you shouldn t let
scary images of witches
on broomsticks
or ghoulish monsters
frighten you
nor should you
worry about such things
as broken mirrors or
black cats crossing your path
as being bad luck either

as far as i m concerned
any cat crossing my path
is bad luck
says i
are you saying you don t

i used to be the most scared
superstitious gypsy moth
in the universe
he said

so how did you overcome it
i asked
how did you get past
all the fear

all the anxiety
and all the looking
over your shoulder

it wasn t easy
nor was it overnight
said he
but you might say
it happened when
i saw the light

saw what light
i asked

the light of jesus
and his love for me

but how can that be—
what is it about jesus love
that sets you free
says me

first of all
he s lord of all
nothing happens
without his call
he s the king of every situation
ain t no surprises at his station
he brings good out of bad
turns your sad
into glad

Spooky Superstitions

jesus is the one who redeems
evil and transforms it into
the things that build us up
and cause us to rejoice inside

you know what
boss
he was right
the church pew underworld
was having a masquerade party today
and i went as an electrified glow worm
i won first prize—
a sleek looking new catamaran—
it s really the cat s meow
boss

amos

Graduation Daze

graduation daze

boss
just seeing all the
young hamsters
and little mice
dressed in their
multicolored cheesecloth
caps and gowns brought
back memories from
many days and gray hairs
gone by

back in sixty-six it was
and there was a song called
quotes here boss
giddy-up giddy-up
four-o-nine
end quotes
roaring up the top forty
mouse music charts

i remember two friends—
steve
a streetwise auto mechanic

mouse
and curt
a cowboy countrified
field mouse—
and i decided to stay up
all night
after our graduation
at bugtussle high

we made a pledge
among ourselves
not to get snookered
into sipping any
high-powered sewer water
but we still had a lot of fun
driving the main drag
from the refrigerator
to the kitchen garbage can
in my shiny fifty-seven cheeserolet

now boss
bugtussle folds up
its ice-cream-stick sidewalks
at ten p m
and by midnight even the
neon lights go out on the
cheese traps

well there we were
at midnight
in the bugtussle diner

listening to four-o-nine
for the twenty-second time
and curt was dying
because he had heard
his favorite song—
i walk the line—
quotes here boss
by johnny bash
the bug in black
only twice the whole night long
and the rest of the diner s customers
were about to drag us out
by our tails

running out of things to do
as well as put-put pellets
for my fifty-seven cheesy
curt had
a brilliant brainstorm
probably his only one all year
to head north for a dip
in big bug lake

we grabbed our multicolored
baggy cheesecloth swim suits
and started for the lake
when we got there
it was about two or three
in the morning
but we didn t care
boss

we jumped in the lake
and splashed and swam
and swam and splashed
until we disturbed a
monstrous mudcat lying on
the lake bottom

we didn t know anything
until he swished by
steve s dangling tail
then he turned
and with a gaping mouth
tried to gulp down curt
and his new cowboy hat
curt always wore his cowboy hat
even while he slept or swam

let s get outta here
boys
curt yelled
but steve and i
were already scrambling
up the rocky shoreline

the mudcat was mad at us
but we didn t care
in fact
we stuck our little
pink tongues at him
boss
as he glided by

when the excitement died down
and we stopped shivering and
shaking from the fright of
our near-death plight
we pitched our terry cloth
tents and promptly went to
sleep—having forgotten all
about our promise to stay
awake all night

two hours later the sun
struck us full in the face
and in our sleepy-eyed
stupor we stared at the
beauty of a yellow-blue-
orangy sunrise shining
all over the place

it was great
boss
and then it struck us—
that sunrise—that
beginning of a brand
new day on the plains—
was like god s sign and
promise to us
that graduation wasn t
an ending
but a brand new beginning
the promise of a life
filled with beauty hope
and joy in jesus

and the bright sun
warming the little whiskers
on our faces
reminded us of his promise
never to leave us
but always to be with us
forever and ever amen

amos

Amos on Perseverance

amos on perseverance

boss
i think i might have
mentioned this before
but life ain t easy
under a church pew

the heathen alley cats
have declared war on me
they climb up on the window ledge
outside the church
and sneer at me
through the stained glass windows
it s unnerving
boss
and sometimes makes
my little tail quiver

and not only that
but the church custodian
is out to get me
i know he is
boss
i keep dodging his mop

but one of these days
he s gonna get me
and i ll be the first
real live waxed mouse
you ve ever seen

oh and then a few days ago
some kids spilled soda
all over the volleyball net
and then stuck it
in a crumpled pile
right behind the storeroom door
so when i dived under the door

to get away from marcellus the cat
i found myself tangled up
in the clutches of a soda
flavored mass of stringy net
so twisted and contorted was i
that my tail was dangling
in front of my whiskers
life can get so sticky sometimes
boss

while i was dangling there
boss
looking more like a pretzel
than a mouse
and needing a sermon

but not really in the mood
to hear one
the lord brought to my mind
the story of milford the millipede
who set sail across the sea
in a large cork

he hollowed out a
little place to sit
while he sailed
and he d drink juice and
eat salt pork
he strapped himself in
with a large padded staple

nothing bothered him
not high winds
nor low ripples

he christened his cork
the unsinkable shepherd
when others scoffed
it ll sink
he replied
absurd

he faced adversity with a
persistent smile
laughed his way
through storms winds and
boredom mile by mile

but his greatest challenge
appeared to be ahead
when an ill-tempered whale
said i ll smash you dead

so the whale flicked his tail
in anger lashed it down
and splashed water all round

but in spite of those blows
milford s cork quickly rose
and floated serenely before
the whale s big nose

said milford to the whale
you can slap and sputter
and frown but you will
never never keep me down

for i m resting on the stuff
that s buoyant enough
to float instead of to drown

sometimes
boss
perseverance simply means
remembering whom
we re resting on

amos

A Tale of Two Frogs

a tale of two frogs

boss
pastor leroy beetle
was a bit discouraged
the other day
he told me
he dreaded the effects of summer
and its warm carefree days
in the church pew underworld

you mean about folks
taking time off for
the weekends
i asked

no not just that
he said
everybody needs
some time away
and off to themselves
even mice and little bugs

so what is there
to cause despair

i said
and stared

everything
and anything
he complained
it s mostly an attitude
in dire need of rectitude

it s a real mindset
against holding pat
everyone bails out
only a few stand stout

surely you re being
unfair in your pity
and despair

not so
he crowed
they run to the beaches
they run to the towns
they run past the leeches
they run with the hounds

with their families
they play
and from the church
they stray
to the movies

A Tale of Two Frogs

they go
and follow the fleshly flow

oh sure they always say
to church i ll come some day
like when hell begins to snow
and it starts to freeze below

with a sigh
he began to cry
amos
said he
please tell to me
as a cheery remedy
the tale of the two frogs

sure
said i
but please don t cry

all right
said he

then listen to me
this tale s
not original with me
for it s copied
you see
from a sermon i did see
so here it be
in all its refinery

the tale of two frogs

two frogs fell into a deep
cream bowl
one was a rather
hardy soul
but the other took a
gloomy view
we shall drown
he cried
without more ado
so with a last despairing cry
he flung up his legs and
said goodbye

quoth the other frog
with a merry grin
i can t get out
but i won t give in
i ll just swim round
till my strength is spent
then will i die the
more content

bravely he swam
till it would seem
his struggles began
to churn the cream
on top of the butter
at last he stopped

and out of the bowl
he joyfully hopped

what of the moral
it s easily found
if you can t hop out
keep swimming round

boss
a bit of commitment
in churning church butter—
that is in service for jesus—
can set life free and
makes the world taste
better to the nth degree
with a seasoning
beyond reasoning
i m sure you ll agree

amos

p s—this story of the optimistic
frog is from knight s master book of
new illustrations published in 1956

Amos Tries to Love His Enemies

amos tries to love his enemies

last sunday pastor leroy beetle
preached about loving your enemies
and turning the other cheek
i wanted to ask
do we have to turn it
even if it s stuffed with cheese
pastor leroy just grimaced
and kept on preaching

jesus said love
your enemies
bless those
who curse you
do good to those
who hate you
and pray for those
who despitefully use you
and try to step on you

does that mean
we have to love those
mean nasty ugly
hateful despicable cats
asked willifred the white rat

yes you do
cats and dogs
birds of prey
and even pesty exterminators
leroy beetle said

it s fortunate
we only have one tail
i whispered to willifred

why is that
he asked

so we don t have to turn
our other tail to the mousetrap
i said

pastor beetle scowled at
us for interrupting his
sermon but i kept
wondering how i was
supposed to love those
awful grab-you-by-the-
throat-and-dangle-you-
over-the-hairy-mouth-
of-hell cats

it was a pure moral
quagmire for me
boss

wouldn t you know it
the first fella i met
coming round the corner
of the churchhouse was
marcellus the mangiest
cat in town
he saw me
when i saw him
i ran hard
but he ran fast
i turned on a whim
but he snared my tail
and things looked pretty slim
boss

well hello there
little mousey
marcellus sneered
and then dangled me in the air
what s up for lunch
he snorted
through his whiskers
how s about some mouse pat-ay
hey hey hey

put me down
you hairy clown i said
almost without thinking
then—of all times—
i remembered pastor leroy
and his sermon

about being kind
to your hairy-footed friends—
that of course is written
with a great deal of sarcasm
boss
so i thought what the heck
i m going to be a speck
in his stomach anyway
so i closed my eyes
and imagined
marcellus to be my mother
i tell you
boss
that s the only way
i could conjure up
any love for the fella

then i said
marcellus
before you gulp me down
and i slide into your
tummy upside down
grant a little mouse s request
and let me make a speech
and a bequest

ok ok i m not a bad guy
he said
you can speak
your piece before you die
he held me high

Amos Tries to Love His Enemies

looked me in the eye
you ve got the floor
just don t badmouth me
or you ll hear me roar
and find yourself
in my smorgasbord

oh i know that
mr marcellus sir
says i
all i wanted to say
was that of all the cats
around us today
you re my favorite one
every day
in fact—and i had to
swallow hard here
boss—
it s an honor to die
in your mouth
sir
and i will do my best
through my sacrificial death
to make your mind more alert
your feet quicker
and your muscles stronger
so you ll be the greatest cat
anywhere around
in short
sir
i just want you to know that

because of my faith in jesus
i love you as my brother cat

boss
i confess i felt
a little like that fella
on the tv beer commercial
who tries to tell everyone
he loves them
but to my surprise
marcellus stared at me
and wiped away a tear
from his green eyes
with the sharpest claw i d
ever seen in my short life

you know what
says he
no one ever told me they
loved me
not even my mother
and certainly
not any mouse about to fall
into my mouth
i think that s the most
wondrous thing
i ve ever heard
do you really mean it
or are you just weird

i started to say
i was a little weird
but then i was filled
with this strange warm glowing
feeling of love
for this mangy cat
who was—and maybe still would
be—my enemy
so
i says
of course i mean
it and not only that
but god loves you too
as sure as the sky is blue

that s amazing
says he
and just to show you
what it means to me
i m going to set you free
not only that but
if i see anyone
messing with thee
they ll have to deal
with me

i nearly passed out
but i hugged the big lout
and do you know
boss

he turned
into the handsomest cat
i d ever seen

i really hate to admit it
boss
but i m going to have
to pay more attention to
pastor leroy—especially
when he s quoting jesus

amos

A Tribute to Howie

a tribute to howie

boss
the other day
i was so depressed
i went to the phone
to call dial-a-mousey-
friend but a recording
came on that said
we re sorry but all our
mousey friends have left
for parts unknown
please call again next
week maybe they ll
be back by then

just when i thought life
and the world in general
had kicked me out of it
boss
i ran across—or
rather stumbled over—
this funny looking little
bookworm named howie
in a local college library

howie was a religion
professor s pet bookworm
and he resided in a corner
of the prof s tottery
old bookshelf

howie has a peculiar
habit for a
religious bookworm
he likes to write
limericks—and
sometimes they don t
even make sense which
makes them even funnier

would you like to
hear a limerick
he asks

no i wouldn t
i reply

ok here s how
it goes
he said
a very near-sighted
old man from drew
made a trip to the
municipal zoo
he mistook a gorilla
for his dear

wife priscilla
and said i thought
you had
shopping to do

i didn t want
to hear it
i yelled

ok here s another
he said
but try to
remember to grin
at the end
a hillbilly singer
named moe
was adept
with his old banjo
he twang and he twang
and sang and he sang
till he died of sadness
and woe

i think i know
how he felt
i said

tell me what you think
of this one
said a green army recruit
willie mill

when asked why he went
over the hill
to avoid being dead
for the sergeant had said
when ready everyone
fire at will

boss
i began to grin
maybe the world
wasn t going to end
i think i had found
a friend so i asked
him to tell me
another one

sure
he said with a smile
but it may take me awhile
oh here s one
the best of the pile
did you hear about the
awful blizzard
it was colder than
a penguin s gizzard
the icicle i ate
i discovered too late
was nothing but a quick-
frozen lizard

boss
i laughed and
i laughed and
it really felt good
it helped me realize
that even if the
whole world rejects me
jesus loves me and his
love through howie
demonstrated the truth of
the proverb that a merry
heart doeth good
like medicine

amos

p s—oh by the way
boss
the limericks were
courtesy of the late dr fred
howard of wayland baptist
university—just thought
you might like to know

Amos Gives Thanks

amos gives thanks

boss
i don t know how life
in downtown whoville
might be around
thanksgiving but life
in bugtussle—the
underground church pew
community—sure ain t
no picnic

who tells the animal
world down here that
thanksgiving is here—
now go out and maim
your fellow animalkind
question mark here
boss
yesterday i jumped in
my little cheese-rolet
for a nice evening
drive around bugtussle
full of joy and gratitude
just for being alive

at a beautiful time of
the year

while i was reflecting
on the wonders of fall
some loon-faced idiot
comes swerving around
pecos bill s bug emporium
and dents my little blue
fifty-seven cheesy
i was a little upset
boss
it really ruined my nice
little fall reverie

i was hopping
up and down
my tail was winding
round and round
and my whiskers
were twitching
up and down
this bozo
was about to get a
piece of my mind and
there was plenty to spare

imagine my surprise
boss
when the loon-faced
idiot turned out to be

pastor leroy beetle
i m so sorry
said he
i was in too much
of a hurry
i didn t see
thee at all

i turned about fifty
shades of red right down
to my pink paw toenails
boss
oh it s okay
pastor leroy says me
i was driving way
too slow for
people on the go

let me pay
for any repairs
says he
it s the least i can
do for thee
and come and have
thanksgiving dinner
with me and the family
say did you see
the lovely fall colors
on the trees and all
the dancing leaves
it s a grand time

of year
don t you think

boss i was so
embarrassed but i
did learn a lesson
it s easy to be thankful when
everything is going great
but tough to do when it ain t
still the lord can make
life better—even amid
the dents and bumps
along the way
the cloudy skies and dreary days
through happy times
and dismal weather
bright smiles and sad letters—
as well as those times
when our faces get redder

amos

A Wart Worries Amos

a wart worries amos

boss
i was looking at my
reflection in the toilet
bowl the other day and
i noticed a growth just
under my whiskers
what is that
i asked myself
and i leaned over
for a closer look
and nearly fell in

it was a wart
exclamation point here
boss
a big fat ugly wart—
i don t think
there are any small
slim and cute ones
anywhere—but there
it was big as life on
my little hairy face

i m ugly
i shouted
to no one in particular
and jumped up and
down and nearly fell
in the bowl again

oh why was i born
with such an
ugly form
i bemoaned
my awful fate
and soon my revulsion
turned to pure hate

i hate you
you re ugly
i told the face in
the toilet bowl
you re no good
you re worthless
you warted soul

in my anger and
despair i didn t see the
lovable slobbery louie
the songdog pad by

why so low, little bro
he cheerily sang

A Wart Worries Amos

oh be like the rain
louie
go away and come again
some other day says me
you always ruin my
moments of misery

can t help it
says he
whatever can the
matter be

i m ugly
as a dry-rotted tree
says me
no one will
love me anymore
when they see me
their eyes turn sore

be careful
little bro
don t stump your toe
or into the water you ll go
louie sang
he was on a roll

you re not ugly at all
for a mouse
you re quite an animal
a delightfully fuzzy

little furrball
louie sang
accentuate the positive
eliminate the negative
i heard that somewhere
he said

remember amos who you are—
not how you look—
and you ll go far
if you re in christ you re a
child of the king
and you re loved by him
who rules everything
you really are special
one of a kind
a greater one of you
you ll never find
you re blessed with
riches the heavenly kind
you re forgiven in christ
and have his mind
your whole life is
filled with peace joy and love
because of jesus and the
father above

so how can you hate yourself
be down and so blue
when you re god s creation
without a doubt it s true

A Wart Worries Amos

you re made perfect in him
not only that
you re empowered by his spirit
and made alive again
he lives in you and you in him
he died for you
forgives your sin
and gives you grace
and peace within
ain t it great
to be one with him

and louie padded on by
while i sat and heaved a sigh
you know
boss
that wart seemed to shrink away
and i thought
what a wonderful day
god s in his heaven
and to me joy has been given

you know
boss
a good
encourager like louie is
worth his weight in cheese

amos

Mystery and Miracle of Christmas, Part One

mystery and miracle of christmas

boss
i was checking on
the specials at sara
spider s underground
discount store the
other day
the moment i stepped
from my snuggly
warm little matchbox
i knew the rat race
was on

crows and magpies were
standing on street corners
hawking their
christmas wares
ratty raccoons and
persnickety pack rats
hornswaggled and hoarded
trash and treasures alike
and not only that
boss
swarms of locusts

grasshoppers lady bugs and
other insects crowded
the bugtussle mall
fur feathers frocks
and flying parts were
scattered in every
direction

i tell you
boss
christmas was lost
somewhere in the
shuffle

all i wanted was a
tiny little red flashing
light to decorate the
top of my christmas
tree sprig
propped against my little
matchbox home
that s all i needed
boss

but what a mess
i was bounced
bumped thumped
shoved and submarined
mostly by a couple of
horned toads
and some loudmouthed

floppy-eared dog
trounced all over
my tail

i started to pout
but i wanted to shout
let me outta here
what s it all about anyway
question mark here
boss

just then sammy
salamander came
wiggling his way
through the crowd
follow me
he said
but i can t wiggle
anything except
my head
i said
cause my tail is dead
never mind that
he said
just go where i go
and be sure to watch
your toes

we wiggled away
far from the mall
to a lonely tableau

under the stars
a manger scene
so alone but
right in the heart
of the town of
bugtussle

jenny my next door
neighbor was playing
mary and willifred the
white rat was joseph
freddy flea played the
role of baby jesus
virgil the praying
mantis was a shepherd
robin redjoy oliver
owl and rawley eagle
were the wise men and
louie the songdog was
a cow

this is a crazy scene
said i
why the strange garb
the fuss and the weird
ceremony—and all of it
so far away from the
malling crowd
what s so all-fired
important you had
to drag me away from my

tiny little red flashing
light for my christmas
tree sprig

sammy just looked at me and
smiled that all-knowing
salamander smile and said
you wanted to know about
christmas—you re standing
at the very heart of its
mystery and miracle right now

the birth of god s
very own son
said louie
most reverently

amos

p s—oops ran out
of room again
boss
sort of like the
innkeeper in bethlehem
but will continue this
glorious tale next time

Mystery and Miracle of Christmas, Part Two

When Amos went shopping for a tiny little red flashing light to decorate the Christmas tree sprig he had propped against his cozy matchbox home, he encountered the trials and tribulations of last-minute Christmas shoppers. In frustration, he called out for the real meaning of Christmas.

About that time, Sammy Salamander wiggled by and pointed him to a little, abandoned nativity scene far from the malling crowd but in the heart of Bugtussle. Jenny (the little girl mouse next door) was playing the role of Mary; Willifred the white rat was Joseph; Freddy Flea was baby Jesus; Virgil the Praying Mantis was a shepherd; Robin Redjoy, Oliver Owl, and Rawley Eagle were the wise men; and Louie the Songdog was a cow.

the mystery and miracle of christmas
part two

sammy just looked at me and
smiled that all-knowing
salamander smile and said
you wanted to know about
christmas—you re standing
at the very heart of its
mystery and miracle right now

the birth of god s
very own son
said louie
most reverently

but how can that be
said me
after all it s plain to see
that baby belongs to she and he

ah that s the mystery of it all
said rawley
looking bigger than tall
you see jesus is god s word
in the flesh

the son of god became
the son of man
robin redjoy sang

divinity took the form
of humanity
virgil noted prayerfully

he became what we are so that
we might become what he is
oliver owl fairly screeched

all right all right
said i
with a frown

i m not deaf—
but i may be now—
so then the mystery of christmas

is the mystery of god
becoming man
louie finished with a flair

the mystery of jesus the god-man
sammy echoed in the night air
as loud as a salamander
would dare

the mystery of his being fully
god yet fully man
said oliver owl
with a certain amount
of dignification
that mystery we
call the incarnation

but what about the miracle
says i somewhat skeptically
you said there was a miracle
with the mystery

so we did and so there is
rawley replied
you see alongside
each of god s mysteries comes
one of his miracles

so what miracle are you
talking about
i said
almost with a shout

the miracle of christmas
my friend
is the virgin birth
he said with a gentle grin

virgin birth
i said
with a certain incredulity
how can that be
is this really necessary for me
to believe
why did it have
to be this way

from the manger scene came
jenny s voice ever so quietly
you see to enter the
world god chose the weakness
of a woman a picture of
submission and humility

and by so doing
virgil added
he eliminated proud
mighty man
from any part
of the plan

let me see if i have this right
said i
groping through the light
god the creator came to his
creation not in power or might
but in the weakness of woman
and the helplessness of a baby
to risk himself in love for all
of us—to love the unlovely and
to die for the ungodly so that
we the unlovely and the ungodly
might live and love forever

boss
that simple tableau speaks
volumes—it s a mystery and
it s absolutely miraculous
but i also learned about
another mystery and miracle
that follows after we accept
the mystery and miracle of
the babe in the manger

that is that god chooses
to live inside each of us
and express his life
through our lives
that s the mystery of godliness—
christ in you
the hope of glory

and the miracle question
mark here
boss—
the miracle we call the new
birth—by simply letting
jesus be born in the manger
of our hearts by faith—
by receiving him as our
savior and lord—we are born
again to live life brand new

and now we can have life
more abundantly by the power
of his spirit flowing freely
after all
it s christ in you and me
the hope of glory
and all eternity

somehow
boss
just saying
merry christmas doesn t
quite do the trick

how about merry christ-in-you
and happy forever

amos

Amos Turns Holiday Glutton

amos turns holiday glutton

boss
this holiday season
got the best of me
i turned into a
cheese-a-holic
i don t know if you
know it or not but
church folk can throw some
outlandish food parties
this time of the year

visions of cheesecakes
cheese crackers
and cheese rolls
danced in my head
on their way to my tummy

it s a joyous time of
the year
says i—
with my mouth stuffed
from ear to ear with a
cheese-filled pear—to
anyone who was near

happy cheese year says
willifred the white rat
as we toasted our
toasted cheese crackers
to each other

i tell ya
boss
it was nearly heaven
on earth
and then at the stroke
of midnight sammy
salamander entered the
church pew underworld
basement door with his
arms loaded down with
cheese pizza—and i
nearly passed out from
sheer delight

now go easy on the
cheese goodies
says pastor leroy beetle
who s quite aware of
my affinity for such
culinary treats
boss

sure pastor leroy
says me
say how would you like

Amos Turns Holiday Glutton

to join me in a cheese
twistie or a cheddar pretzel

you re going to turn
into a cheddar pretzel
he warned
you d better
go sleep it off in the barn

party pooper
says me to him
and i went back to get
my fill of a cheese-filled
croissant

finally the party and
the flowing cheese river
ended and i gently tucked
my overextended tummy into
my little matchbox bed

ah now for a long
winter s nap
says me
but alas it wasn t
to be
i tossed and i turned
my stomach roiled and burned
i broke out in sweats
and i shivered with the cold
my head ached

and my tummy reeled
and rolled

about that time
louie the songdog
padded by
my little matchbox pad
and heard my groaning
and moaning

whatsa matter little guy
says he
with a twinkle
in his eye
it sounds like
a war going on there
need any help or a
little cheer

my tummy is
keeping me awake
it s putting me
in an awful state

when louie asked me
what i ate
boss
his eyes rolled
to the back of
his shaggy
head

amos
says he
don t you know
the bible warns
against that sort of thing

but i just was having fun
lamented me

but it s not fun now is it
says he
god doesn t give us
these warnings to take
away our fun
but to make our life better
to give us joy in the sun

he was right
boss
gluttony
is a cheesy way to live
life sure feels better when
you follow god s way

amos

The Holiday Cheese Run-off

the holiday cheese run-off

boss
i guess you heard
about my holiday cheese binge
the mouthy magpies and
busybody blue jays
can t seem to find anything else
to talk about this week

they could chirp and
chortle all they wanted to
about my eating habits
boss
and it wasn t a problem
for me until just the other
day when i nearly got stuck
in the mouse hole in the
corner of the choir loft

it was an ugly sight
boss
my rear end was shakin
to beat the band just to
get my body unstuck from
that hole in the wall

i finally did get unstuck—
thanks to louie the songdog
who lassoed my foot
and yanked
with all his hairy might
i m not sure
boss
but i think my left hind leg
is now a bit longer
than my other three
i feel a little like the drunk guy
walking along the curb—one
foot in the street and one
on the curb—and wondering
why the world is tilted

i tell ya
boss
i needed to
go on a super-duper
exercise program
one that would trim
and tone my
little fat mousy hide

i recalled running
around a mousetrack in
high school—scenes of
fellow runners cavorting
in the bugtussle marathon—
what scintillating specimens

The Holiday Cheese Run-off

of athletic prowess
exclamation point here
boss

so running became my goal
in life i was going
to get in shape
no more flubby
tubby for me
i had visions of myself
as a supercharged
lean mean mouse machine

come on
boss
humor me
at least quit snickering
under your breath

early the next morning
i donned my cheesecloth
jogging suit and charged
around the loop in the
church s fellowship hall—
for about twenty paces
that is—i tripped over a
wadded-up church bulletin
and landed smack dab on
my chin whiskers
so i decided to run a
loop around the church s

rose garden but i kept
being bombarded
by a band of
nose-diving mosquitoes
i ran harder
but it was no use
i was too easy a target

i cowered behind an
old dead tree stump
and tried to retrieve
my breath and any
movable muscles
i can t make it
i muttered to myself
when i thought
no one was listening

about that time sammy
salamander waddled by and
says why don t you try what
the indians used to do when
they ran long distances

what s that
says me
in a wheezing whisper

each runner would put a
small smooth round stone
in his mouth and suck on it

to keep his mouth moist
while he relaxed and ran
says sammy matter-of-factly

okay says i and
boss
i tried it
but while i was running
and turning a corner marcellus
the ugly ungodly cat pounced
at me out of nowhere—and i
swallowed the little round
pebble—it choked me up
boss

the next sunday morning pastor
leroy beetle preached on first
timothy four-eight that says
physical training is of some
value but godliness has value
for all things
exercise is good but
seeking god is greater
says he

and all i could do was mutter a
resolute and contrite amen

amos

Amos Falls into a Vat of Chocolate

amos falls into a vat of chocolate

boss
i was just minding my
own business the other day
jogging across the church s
kitchen counter when my
little mousy toes tripped
over a chocolate-covered
spatula and i fell headlong
into a bigger-than-life
bowl of chocolate

it was horrible
boss
i came up sputtering and
gagging and my whiskers
were dripping continuously
with the dark syrupy mess

it was at that point that
little ryan rabbit came
hopping by
with his fuzzy mother
look mommy it s

one of those chocolate-
covered easter bunnies
he said

no dear it s not
his mother replied
come on we ve got
to hop along

but mommy
why don t we stop
little ryan said

Amos Falls into a Vat of Chocolate

maybe he ll give us some easter
eggs—hey mister easter
bunny will you give me
an easter egg all chocolaty
and pure

no but if you come any
closer i ll give you a lump
on the noggin
that s for sure
now go away and
leave me alone
let me pine away my miserable
life in this chocolaty manure

he sure is a grumpy
easter bunny
says ryan
as he hopped merrily away

then freddie the flea
came upon the scene and
wanted to rescue me
boss
i ll save you
amos
i ll save you
he says
and off he goes to find
his flea-size scout rope

meanwhile i m making
chocolate soap bubbles and
wondering why this stuff
doesn t taste any better

here i am
don t worry
amos
freddie said as he tossed
the rope into the vat
but he forgot to tie it to the faucet
or anywhere so when he tried
to pull me up out of the goo
he and the rope fell into it too

i searched around
in the dark gooey mass
and found freddie floundering
and going down fast
so i picked him up with my
long flowing tail and set him
up on the sink close to the rail

some passers-by saw freddie
and said
hey look at that—a
chocolate-covered flea
must be one of those
richer varieties

Amos Falls into a Vat of Chocolate

just then sammy salamander
came by and said
why do you get all the fun
amos and dove right into
the middle of me
and the chocolate
hey this is great
he says
then looks at me
whatza matter can t you
do the back stroke like me
says he

no i can t do the back stroke
says me
and besides i don t
want to do the back stroke
can t you see
that i m drowning
in this chocolate sea

oh sorry i thought you were
playing like me
says he
do you want to get out

oh no why should i want out
i said sarcastically
i thought i would dive down
and touch the bottom

of the bowl and then see
how much chocolate i could
stuff in my ears
how about that huh

yeah that sounds like fun
says sammy
and down he went to
the bottom of the bowl
but i don t think
i have any ears
he moaned

never mind
i shouted
get me outta here
but it didn t do any good
boss
he was on his
way to the bottom of the
bowl again

just then louie the songdog
padded by
hi amos
looks
like you got chocolate
all over you
how about a big
ol sloppy lick
he asks

Amos Falls into a Vat of Chocolate

louie
just get me outta
here ok and you can have
all the licks you want
says me desperately

ok here goes
and he picks me up
by the tail and holds me
over his mouth with chocolate
dripping off my little
soggy whiskers

mm good
louie said
as he slurped me up one
side and down the other

boss
i normally would not like
being a doggie popsicle
but this time i couldn t
have been happier
i gave the flop-eared louie
a big ol mousy kiss and
went running deliriously
in search of the nearest
bird bath

to quote a famous movie
guy by the name of amos

gump or something
life is like a big bowl of
chocolate cause you never
know how it s gonna turn out—
it can be sweet
or you can drown in it

amos

Sidney Seeks God

sidney seeks god

one evening last week
boss
i bumped into a
little flashing red light
it was sidney the shutterbug

i m on my way to
find god
says he
so i thought i would
start at the church
pew underworld
church house but
nobody s there—not
even pastor leroy beetle

i m here
says me

oh you don t count
says he
you re always
here like last year s

old shoes whether we
need you or not—you re
not at all like god

thanks a lot
says me
you ve really made my day
sid
now why don t you go away

oh you know what i mean
says he
but he flew away anyway

boss
he flew from one place to
another without much success
he flitted from one religious
function to another
he cried at bugtussle s
biggest funerals
he dodged rice at bugtussle s
finest society weddings
but still god was nowhere
in sight

sidney flew from the
grandest cathedrals
to the lowliest tents
and god was either

Sidney Seeks God

coming or god had
already went

god was nowhere to
be found neither in
the country nor in the
big bad town

sidney then tried to join
the french flying—
not frying
boss—
legion but
they were looking for
dive-bombing mosquitoes
so he went to join the
navy sea bees but he
couldn t pass as an
underwater flying bee

he was hoping to find
god in the trenches and
the horrors of war-is-hell
fighting but to no avail

finally
boss
sid flittered home
discouraged and
despairing of his quest

oh where is god
he moaned and wailed
i ve searched in the
highest heavens and
even in the lowest hell

but then along came sally
the lowly sugar ant
who was weeping and crying
over her fate in life

no one cares about me
cried she
look at the state of my misery
i m down and out
not a penny to count
no bread or food
tell me
then where s the good

sally dragged all six
of her legs
no one cares
there s no light to see
no way for me

but then she looked up and
saw the flickering flashes
of sid s little light

oh what a pretty sight
how lovely and bright
sally cried with delight
god still loves me
god still cares—
to send someone
with such a cheerful flare

and somehow
boss
sidney understood that god
was there all along
and didn t need to be found—
after all he wasn t lost—
he just needed to be
seen with the eyes of faith

you know
amos
sidney said to me
it s a mistake to think that god
is only—or even chiefly—
concerned with religion

he is the essence of life love
joy and serenity

amos

The Spaghetti Dive

the spaghetti dive

boss
there s a new form of
high-class entertainment
here in the church pew
underworld these days—
naw it s not roping wild
aphids or dunking
millipedes or trying to
catch greased pot-bellied
pigs—as much fun as
all that sounds

the young daredevils of the
church kitchen are calling it
the spaghetti dive and all the
church pew crew now flock
to the top of the water faucet to
dive into the church s leftover
sunday night spaghetti
and meatball dinner

it all started by accident or
at least by drunkenness

rudy the sewer rat thought
he was a high-wire circus
performer tiptoeing along
the edge of the kitchen sink
when he missed a step and
fell headlong into the bowl

help help
says he
in between gurgles of
spaghetti sauce

it wasn t long
boss
before
a crowd began to gather
around the sink s edge
hey looky there rudy
swimming in the spaghetti
hey rudy whatcha doing

help help was all the
drunken sewer rat could
utter but nobody heard
him through all the sauce

that looks like fun
says sammy salamander
let s dive in too last one
in is a grumpy old toad

The Spaghetti Dive

so
boss
they all dived in
and rudy nearly drowned
in all the splashing
but he was happy
he thought it was the
biggest rescue party
he d ever seen

that s how this ungodly
craze started
boss
and
now freddy flea and
sammy are daring me
to do the dive

some of the more fearless
ones were jumping off
the high dive—the top of
the faucet—complete with
somersaults flips and twists
it was an awesome sight
boss
but not for me

still they kept taunting me
and urging me to do it
finally against my better
judgment and the little

spirit voice inside me
i caved in to the pressure

teetering on the edge of
the kitchen sink i squinted
into the yawning blood-red
spiraling abyss of
spaghetti hell

i was about to turn
around and walk
determinedly back home
when my little mousy toes
slipped and i did a
sprawling double-back
flip over into the
looming pasta bowl
amid hoots and hollers
and oohs and aahs

i landed with an
ungraceful splash and
a ricocheting meatball
thunked me on the head

boss
i was sinking
the spaghetti strands
closed around me
dragging me
down down down

i gasped for air and all i
could pray was father
don t let me be entangled
in bondage again

the lord must have heard
me through my spurts and
gurgles because suddenly
louie the songdog s big
smiling hairy jowls
grabbed me by the nape
of my neck
pulled me up out of
the spaghetti mire
and set my little feet on
the solid kitchen counter
i kissed it twice
boss
and the dog once

amos

p s—louie the songdog
looks a lot like jesus
to me now
boss

Amos Bells the Cat

amos bells the cat

marcellus the mangy
ungodly cat has been
running amuck here
boss
terrorizing little mice
hamsters guinea pigs and
even experimental white
rats like willifred

it s crisis of
biblical proportions
cried henny-penny
who had just escaped from
the-sky-is-falling insane
asylum for lunatic chicks
it s raining cats and dogs
minus the dogs
lamented the addled chicken
the sky is falling again
the sky is falling again

bertie woeworm just happened
to be wiggling by

and he took up the refrain
the cats are coming
the cats are coming
woe is us
woe is us
the sky is overflowing
with flying cats
oh woe is us
we ll all soon be mush

things were getting a little
out of hand
boss
even sammy salamander
was sobbing wherever he swam
and little dewey duck was wringing
his webbed feet in despair

so
boss
at our next meeting
of the wishy-washy american
rodent and toad society—warts—
willifred the white rat enumerated
marcellus the cat s heinous crimes—
scaring little baby rats
chasing elderly mice
unmercifully scraping his claws
across linoleum kitchen floors
in the dead of night
screeching and howling with his buddies

in the alley after midnight
and worst of all sneaking up on
poor helpless critters when they
least suspect dire danger
anywhere around

what will we do
where will we go
there s no place to run
no place to hide
a chorus of baby rats cried

then willifred the white rat
recalled a remark that
theophilus the noble first-
century cat offered about
how to handle troublesome
obnoxious twenty-first century cats

if you re having trouble
with a renegade cat just put
a bell around his neck and
you ll always know
where he is
it s as simple as that

and
boss
all the warts members
voted unanimously to bell
ol marcellus and make life

better for everyone
the only problem was who
would be the poor
unfortunate soul to do
the deed—and wouldn t you
know it
boss
i drew the
short straw

with bell in tow i tiptoed
straight to the nefarious lair
of marcellus but
he wasn t there
ok so i get to go home
says me to myself
but then willifred s voice
came floating
through the air
we re counting on you
amos
don t fail us

so i set up an ambush
just above the cushion
where marcellus sleeps
i nearly fell asleep
waiting for that mangy
cat to show up and then
when he did i nearly died

after the monster finally
settled in and closed his
eyes i quietly lowered my
little lasso with the bell
attached but it hit him in
the nose and the ringing
of the bell woke him up

he chased me into the
nasty old cat litter box
and i went up and out
on top but then i tripped
and fell on
the cat s backside
i jumped down
just in time to avoid
his swatting claws but
when i turned and looked
back my lasso with its bell
had looped itself around
marcellus s tail

the cat was belled
exclamation point here
boss

now the tolling of
the bell signals peace
in our time—at least in the
church pew underworld

amos

Amos on Spring

The coming of spring caught Amos somewhat off guard this year. He was still anticipating snowstorms that never came, when the first wildflower poked its multicolored head out of the ground. Though amazed at the sight, Amos went on his way without giving it much thought.

So spring sprang on him by surprise. He stumbled into it the other day when he met Robin Redjoy.

amos on spring

boss
this has been a
dull dreary week
even the sun
didn t want to come
out and play until
the other day

i was down and out
boss—
lower than
a caterpillar s belly
nothing could cheer me
up not even peanut
butter and jelly

then along came robin
singing like the entire
london philharmonic
his voice—in place
of his reputation—
preceded him

it was pure
unadulterated
high-spirited joy
boss
and it grated on
my misery

solomon once wrote
in proverbs twenty-five verse twenty—
as he that taketh away a
garment in cold weather
and as vinegar upon
nitre so is he that
singeth songs to an
heavy heart—i knew
what the man was
talking about
boss
robin was pouring
vinegar on my nitre—
whatever that is

but before i could
either grump or
quote scripture to him
boss
mopey molerus—the
downcast and despondent
mole—you remember him
boss
he s the lowest mole
on the totem pole
in the bottom hole
anywhere around

anyway mopey pushed
his head out of the
ground and looked
everywhere around
and said
what s all this
i ve never been
here before
where s the dirt
maybe i m at the earth s core

robin redjoy though
was halfway through
the hallelujah chorus
boss
singing the
joys of spring
with a cheerful heart

it was beginning
to become a bit
contagious even
in spite of my
stubbornness

how dull life is
said mopey mole
this world is just a
dirty hole
i eat i dig and i store
and all i find is a bore

robin sang high in
the blue—
how sweet is the
morning dew
how clear the brooks
how fair the flowers
i rejoice in this
world of ours

mopey asked what s this
chirp-and-shout
tell me what s all the
fuss about

o the sunshine and the
pine trees
the green grass white clouds
and blue seas

spring
said robin in his big oak tree
gives to the world such
grace and beauty

nonsense
said mopey the molerus
i ve lived in this
world more than youse—
tunneled it and traveled
through it—i ve sniffed
snorted smelled
and chewed it—and i tell ya
there ain t nothing to it
cept great big gobby
fishing worms through it

boss
it just goes to
show you how a fella s
perspective can color
his whole world

amos

Amos Meets Dewey Duck

amos meets dewey duck

boss
i ran into dewey duck
the other day
you remember dewey
he wanted to be a
business duck
start a cracker factory
and make his first million
before he molted
but the lord
called him to be a
missionary evangelist
just in the nick of time—
and saved the world from
a mass production of
quacker-crackers

anyway
boss
dewey was
waddling around the streets
aimlessly when he bumped
into me

hey what s the matter
with you dewey
you nearly crumpled my
little whiskers
says me

oh sorry
says he
i m just having a
misery kind of day

why what s happened
says i

do you think the lord
speaks to folks in dreams
says he

of course
says me
the bible always talks
about dreams and visions
but you have to be careful
ya gotta be sure
it s from the
lord and not satan
or the pizza from the
night before

i m pretty sure it s
from the lord

Amos Meets Dewey Duck

says he
but it s more like a
nightmare than a
dreamlike prophecy

well tell me about it
says me

not much to tell
says he
except in my dream
all i could see was
the heathen alley
cats falling into hell

great
says me

no it ain t
says he

what do you mean
says me again

i mean the lord says
for me to go there
and

go where

go there and preach to
the heathen alley cats
says he

you re crazy
says me
surely the lord hates
those alley cats the
same as we

no i don t think he does
says he
the lord says
they re creatures
he s made the same as
you and me
and i m supposed to go
there because
he loves them too—
just like he
loves me and you

no no maybe you can
make a deal with the
lord tell him you ll go
anywhere but there

i tried that but the lord
said his place of blessing
protection power peace

Amos Meets Dewey Duck

and presence is there—
and there alone

well maybe you can
stay here instead
tell him you ll do
anything here but just
don t send you there

no i tried that too
but he wouldn t listen
he just said
that wouldn t do
then he reminded me of
the story of elijah and the
ravens by the brook cherith
in first kings seventeen

what did he say
says me

he said the ravens would
not have fed elijah
anywhere else but there
and later the widow would
not have appeared
anywhere else except at zarephath
in sidon

but what does that mean
says me

well god didn t say
elijah ramble around
just as you please and i ll
provide for you
and elijah didn t say
here god i m going over
here and you follow along
and provide for me
instead god said
go there

but what s so special
about there
says me

there was the place of
god s will for elijah
says dewey
there is the place of god s
purpose god s power and
god s provision
and that s what god told
me—that i have to go
there to the alley cats

well
boss
that s exactly
what little brave dewey
duck did—and
it was amazing
it was unbelievable

a revival broke out
among those heathen
alley cats—they
weren t heathen
anymore—they
repented and cried
out to god
for mercy and grace
there was wailing
and weeping
all over the place

it was a sight to see
all those cats down
on their knees
in fact they pledged
to go on mouse- and
duck-free diets and
nearly all have sworn
to veggie-only bites

what a miracle
boss
what power—all because
of a god who cares
and a duck who dared
to go when god said there

amos

p s—i m sure god has a
there for each of us
somewhere he wants us
to be
something he wants us
to do
may he find in us a willing
heart and faith enough
to dare to be there

Louie's Supper Technique

louie s supper technique

boss
you remember louie
the songdog who s always
so happy and wags his big
hairy tail everywhere
question mark here

well louie has a peculiar
habit that several of us
have noticed
from time to time
i know i know
all of us in the church
pew underworld
have peculiar habits
at feeding time
you were going to say
weren t you
boss
another question mark

but louie s actions seem
to take on larger-than-
life significance

if you know
what i mean

here s the deal
every evening at
suppertime louie used
to feed at the kitchen
table when the preacher
and his wife would sit
down to eat but apparently
one day the preacher s wife
objected—i think it was
right after louie gobbled
up half a roast that the
missus had spent half
the day cooking

anyway somehow louie
sensed the reason for
being refused food
while the preacher s
family were enjoying
their meal together

louie s smarter than his
floppy ears and hairy
jowls look
boss
and hunger is a mighty
powerful motivation
in the animal world

so louie would crawl
under the table when
the preacher s wife
wasn t looking and
then he would sit with
his nose resting on the
preacher s knee

oh it was a pitiful
sight to see
boss

but the silent expectant
faith of that dog s
appeal was too much
for the preacher—and
when his wife wasn t
watching the preacher
would slip choice tender
morsels of food under
the table and into louie s
eager waiting mouth

it became the marvel of
the church pew underworld

others of us have tried to
duplicate louie s supper
table technique boss but
not always with the
same success

somehow the nose of a
centipede or a tarantula
or even a salamander
doesn t have quite the
same appeal that a big
hairy sad-eyed dog does

but of course that s not
the real point of this tale
boss

louie s nose resting
expectantly on his
master s knee is the
perfect epitome of our
reaching up to god in
faith fully anticipating
his best and knowing
wholeheartedly that he
will never ever fail

god is so good
he provides for our
every need and for
our daily cheese—as we
say in our paraphrase of
the lord s prayer—
may our faith rest on him
implicitly like louie s nose
on the preacher s knee

amos

The Rose of Suffering Love

As Easter nears, Amos, the poetic churchmouse, has been intensely reviewing the devastating events of the first Good Friday in history.

The agony of the Savior in Gethsemane; the kiss of betrayal by one of His own; the mockery and injustice of a kangaroo court; the beating, the taunting, and the scourging by the Roman soldiers; and finally, the cruel, tortuous nailing of His body to the cross to die has completely overwhelmed the little churchmouse's soul and intellect.

In a cover letter to his column this week, he writes:

such agony is
unutterable
incomprehensible
unbearable to even
think about

and to think
boss
that my sin
caused
his pain
to begin with

it just makes me
hurt inside out

With that note, Amos turned away from the
church office's old computer, and he stumbled through
the rows of church pews and out into the church's rose
garden in the front courtyard.

Being in a reflective mood, he immediately bumped
into a rosebush, complete with sharp thorns.

the rose of suffering love

boss
i guess you
heard about the
rosebush incident
how can something
so beautiful
hurt so badly
question mark
i m still
picking thorns
out of my tail
it s not funny
boss
whiney the porcupine
still chuckles when
he sees me
it s the first time
he s grinned in
seven months
he says

The Rose of Suffering Love

but i ve been thinking
boss
about that rose
and its thorns
it has a message
even to the one
who scorns

so here s a poem
to the rose of
suffering love
dedicated to our
divine sufferer
above

tucked beneath the beauty
of a rose
hides the throbbing torture
of the thorn
guarding love s soft petals
from its foes
that green sentinel watches
night and morn

he who would embrace that
beauteous rose
often pays the price of
wounded love
to touch where beauty s
sweet fragrance grows
he mingles his love with
sorrow s blood

the creator shaped a world
of grace
a grand garden of roses
and love
but then sin raised up its
hellish face
coating the earth with death
like a flood

beauty s roses wilted in
disgrace
sin thrust out its
treacherous thorn-club
yet god sent his son—the
cross to face—
to mingle his love with
sorrow s blood

with his precious life-blood
flowing down
jesus trimmed that thorn-club
to a nub
and caused grace and mercy
to abound
by mingling his love with
sorrow s blood

amos

Amos on Easter

amos on easter

boss
it s here
exclamation point
the greatest time of
the year—easter—
it s the time for lilies
green grass
little bunnies and chicks
multicolored eggs
and bright butterflies
symbols of brand-new lives
in jesus the messiah

sometimes though
boss
i wonder what that
first easter must have
been like
you know
what those bible characters
really felt and thought—

and how we might have
acted in their place
would we have understood
his act of grace
or would we instead
have sought to save our face
question mark

boss
i went to bed in my
matchbox last night musing
over what it might have
been like as a bedouin
mouse in jesus day
and immediately the
sandman dumped a
whole truck load on
me and i drifted into
a dreamland of dusty
arabic deserts where
i was trudging my way
into jerusalem

just as i neared the
outskirts of the city
it seemed as if all of
creation was coming
alive in mourning
tears flowed from
cracks in disjointed
rocks making wet

tracks in the dirt
flowers closed their
blooms and grapes
and pomegranates
bowed their fruitful
heads in shame
a weeping willow
sobbed uncontrollably
beside the road

what s the matter
says i
what s caused
you so to cry

why haven t you heard
says she
all about black friday
the day the darkness
ruled over the sun at
noon the day the
earth quaked
the rocks broke
the thunder roared and
the lord spoke
where on earth were
you—in kalamazoo

no i don t think so
says i

but tell me why
all these wonders
on the land
and in the sky

the rose of sharon has died
she replied
and there s no place to hide
so all we ve done is cried
and cried and
cried and cried

i still don t understand
says i
who s the rose
of sharon and why
did he die

she said he s the
rose of love
sent from the lord above
in him dwelt the
beauty of flowers
everywhere he was
the fairest of ten
thousand anywhere
he was perfect
said she
he radiated glory
peace life and victory

but why oh why

said i
did such a
great rose die

he was despised and
rejected of plants
there were those who
wished to kill him
and dance
on his grave and
just leave him
for the ants

but again
said i
why

a sad lily nearby
offered me this reply
his beauty angered
the thornbushes
and thistles
said she
compared to him
their glory
was turned
to ugly
through hot-tempered jealousy
and green-leafed envy

yes that s right said
the sorrowful willow
they tore at his
green leaves
they pierced his
peaceful petals
lashed at his lithe stem
plucked his life up
by the roots
strapped him to a stake
and hung him out
to dry—and die

then the willow began
to wail and the
lily began to lament
oh he s gone
she mourned and cried
he s nowhere around
his life-juices poured
out on barren unfeeling
ground

wait said a flit
flashing by
now what was that
said i

just me said barry
the bumblebee but
listen i ve got some news

that ll set you free
you see i ve been
talking to the marigold
planted next to the garden
tomb and she told
me that the rose of
sharon is alive and whole
in fact he s touched
her and brought new life
to her soul

oh joy he s alive
the weeping willow sang
he s alive
the lily trumpeted the refrain
he s alive to live
forevermore buzzed barry
by his death he buried
death in the deepest sea
and by his life he
lives to set his flowers
free

by then
boss
we were
all shouting hallelujah
hallelu when the sun
peeped through those
stained-glass windows
and glory covered

my little matchbox bed
what a way to wake
to easter
boss

amos

Amos Visits Kinfolk

With the coming of spring and the annual dust bowl weather on the Plains, Amos started feeling lonely. Every time he saw a little daisy sprouting through the ground or the tender young grass blades blowing in the wind, he became more and more homesick to see some of his family—especially his little niece, Annie Marie.

amos visits kinfolk

boss
i guess you heard
that i was trying to
leave town on the next
mouse train

it s true
i ve packed
my samsonite cheesecloth
traveling bags and i m
on my way to the
bugtussle train station

i can t wait to see
some of my country
cousin field mice in

house melrose muleshoe
and some even in the
faraway stretches of
the texas panhandle

but the one i really
want to see is my
little niece annie marie
i tell you
boss
she sets the prairie
ablaze with her mousy
beauty and youthful
joie de vivre

Amos Visits Kinfolk

but
boss
when she looks
up at me with those
big brown eyes
my old gray whiskers
droop to the floor
and soon i m playing
horsey or hide-and-seek
or cheeseball keepaway

or sometimes we ll
just sit on a couple of
padded thimbles and
watch big bird and bert
and ernie on sesame
street

so boss as i sit in the
bugtussle train
station waiting for
the midnight mouse
express it seemed so
natural just to grab
a notepad and pen
and jot down a little
poem for annie marie

ode to annie marie
(with apologies to
sesame street)

once upon a
snuffle-up-a-gus
there was a
russle-on-a-mus
now he was kin to a
rhine-os-a-pot-a-mus
but he was such an
awful-little-cuss
and mean as an ornery
hic-a-pus

but one day while riding on his
snuffle-up-a-gus
he decided to jump off and hop
on a hustle-bustle-bus
you see he wanted to stir up
a rumple-stumple-fuss
and chew on some
fuzzy-ruffle-stuff

but when he jumped on the
hustle-bustle-bus
his tail-er-ron-a-mus
got stuck in the swinging
swack-a-sore-e-us
and he yelled to high
hassel-dor-e-us
and never again was he a mean
and ornery hic-a-pus
but he was the nicest
russel-on-a-mus

to ever ride on a
snuffle-up-a-gus

amos

p s—boss
sometimes it
takes a little pain to
straighten us out and get
us back on the right path
again as the russel-on-a-mus
found out in the poem
i ll be back next time
be sure to keep the
coffee brewing
i think i ll take
your suggestion and
try a little sugar and
creamer in it because
it still makes my
tail too kinky

Attack of the Birds

the attack of the birds

boss
there have been
some strange air currents
passing through the church
pew underworld these days

in alfred hitchcock style
the birds have landed and
they re causing more
ruckus than an octopus
on a merry-go-round

first came the parrots
who repeat what others
say—have you heard
what so-and-so said—
they re the ones who
always cry—they say
they say—and
boss
their gossipy ways may
completely undermine
the church pew family

then came fauntleroy the
fan-tailed pigeon who
strutted all through the
underworld flashing his
pinfeathers and wanting
to be the focus of
attention but
boss
all he managed to do was
cause confusion disgust
and jealousy

but fauntleroy was
nothing compared to
horace the hawk whose
sharp eyes never missed
a fault committed by
pastor leroy beetle
the songbird choir
and any church pew member
horace always preyed on
the helpless and he
usually sat by himself
in the corner pew

then the jay birds came
in a bunch fussing
chattering screeching to
high heaven and making
a hell on earth

after them came
the bats
the old hypocrites
in the bird family—
the bat looks
like a bird from one
angle and a rodent
from another
he has wings
but looks like a rat
the only difference is
the way you look at him
boss

then in the stealth of the
night—along with the bats—
flew in the crows
the undercover agents
who steal another s corn
crows are spiritual thieves
always trying to steal
someone else s blessing
and by the way
boss
crows sure make a lot of
noise when they re caught

finally
boss
there came the swans
those beautiful birds

who have no certain
dwelling place but just
float from church pew
to church pew
swans always
look for a better pond
but are never satisfied

just when we thought the
church pew underworld
would be overwhelmed by
our frantic feathered foes
there were two other birds
who showed up in the
nick of time—
first the turtle dove
the bird of peace
rest beauty and security
the promise of god s love
on the way

then
boss
in majestic style
rawley eagle swooped down
out of heaven as it were
soaring high
diving hard and fast
driving the church s
enemies out and bearing
healing in his wings for those

Attack of the Birds

wounded by those hapless
bird brains

god s might and power
flew in the wake of rawley s
wings and the church pew
underworld—even to a
woeworm—rejoiced

amos

Lefty
the Lightning Bug

lefty the lightning bug

we have a radical left-wing
lightning bug terrorizing
the church pew underworld
boss
and it s driving a few
of us more insane
than usual

of course with his being
left-wing-ed that means
that he generally flies in
circles but they re really
weird circles boss

in fact there s a faction
of us who suspect that
lefty the left-wing-ed
lightning bug may be
responsible for those
weird circles in peru and
corn field patterns in
other parts of the earth
but that s just speculation

still we all know lefty
has been known to dive
bomb into liquor bottles—
and you know how
dangerous it is to mix
lightning bugs with any
sort of alcohol
boss

well lefty began flying
zig-zaggedy patterns
complete with flashing
tail lights and notorious
dive bombings here in the
church pew underworld
and it has created all sorts
of panic pathos
and pandemonium
boss

dora the little duckling came
quacking to her mother
that she was attacked by
a flashing ufo flying upside
down over the duck pond
then willie the wiggleworm
crashed into a boulder while
he was trying to dodge
lefty s terroristic dive run

Lefty the Lightning Bug

the final straw however
came when lefty tried to
disrupt pastor leroy beetle s
sunday sermon by flashing
patterns of six-six-six in the air
over the bugtussle choir

just then big rawley eagle
swooped down from the
clouds and into the church
pew underworld meeting place

the wind from his gigantic
wings toppled little lefty the
lightning bug flippety-side-up

what was that
says he
in awed incredulity
was that a space ship
or alien entity

naw
that was only me
says rawley
as he landed
just above the baptistry

you scared the be-jeebers
out of me

says lefty rather timidly
why did you do that
to little bitty me

well i didn t mean to harm
you little one
but don t you see
what evil you ve done
to these friends of mine
how they run and hide
from your wacky aerial signs
and your dangerous flight
patterns and designs

you re only creating
confusion and despair
with your flashing tail
and your nonsensical dives
through the air

lefty lowered his head and his
wings and asked softly
what can i do to make amends
for all my flings

repent and ask for forgiveness
and a change you will see
says rawley
jesus will come in and
set you free

you ll be a blessing to others
you ll see
and a light to shatter
the darkness of life s futility

amos

The Nothingness Sermon

the nothingness sermon

the great preacher
the rev benton
the black labrador
delivered last
sunday s sermon
boss
and the whole
church pew underworld
was present
it was great

he preached a message on
creation and nothingness
that god had created the world
out of nothing

here s how it came across
boss

when heaven and earth
was yet unmade
says benton
when there was empty

blackness and void
formlessness and darkness
was on the face
of the deep
when time was yet unknown—
thou in thy bliss and majesty
did live—and love alone

he called light out of darkness—
he called cosmos out of chaos—
he called order out of confusion

but the question still clamors
for an answer—where did god
come from—
well the answer is—he came
from nowhere—
now that s theologically correct
and it s biblically sound
for habakkuk said i saw him
when he left the hills of teman—
the holy one from mount paran—
and teman simply means
nothing and nowhere—
so he came from nowhere

i made that statement in the
church pew underworld in
detroit some time ago
and a big bug came to talk
with me after the meeting

The Nothingness Sermon

he said to me
preacher
let s be reasonable
about this thing
you were up there talking about
god came from nowhere
and that doesn t make sense
let s be reasonable about it

i said
all right if you want to
be reasonable about it—the
reason god came from nowhere
is there wasn t anywhere for
him to come from

and coming from nowhere
he stood on nothing
and the reason he had to
stand on nothing is there was
nowhere for him to stand

and standing on nothing
he reached out where there
was nowhere to reach
and caught something when
there was nothing to catch

and hung something on
nothing—and told it to
stay there

now you ll find that in job
twenty-six verse seven that
he hung this world on nothing

and standing on nothing
he took the hammer of his own
will and he struck the anvil
of his omnipotence and sparks
flew therefrom
and he caught them on the tips
of his fingers and flung them
into space—and bedecked
the heavens with stars

and nobody said a word
the reason nobody said anything
there wasn t anybody there to
say anything

so god himself said that s good

amos

p s—that s from a message
delivered by the great pastor
dr s m lockridge at the new
mexico baptist evangelism
conference in january 1981

Greed Strikes Willifred

greed strikes willifred

boss
i talked willifred the white
rat into taking a trip in his
newfangled tiny
time traveler machine
all we have to do is
just strap it onto my fifty-seven
cheese-rolet matchbox car

where do you want to go
amos says he
i can take you
to the edges of history
just watch me and see

let s take a trip to the
sea of galilee
sometime around the end
of the first century
says me

you bet
says he

just let me fiddle with
the dates a bit
and we ll be there
in the flick of a flit

sure enough
boss
that
little machine rattled and
rumbled and when it
stopped we stepped out
facing the sea of galilee

just then a little hairy
goat ambled up to us
and gently bellowed
hey you guys are late
the tour s nearly over

what tour
says me

the archaeological tour
of where jesus and his
disciples used to roam
and how he would feed
thousands of people with
just a little boy s lunch of
loaves and fishes

have they found any
archaeological evidence
says willifred the white rat
who used to be a mad
scientist s experimental
lab animal

nothing but a few rusty
fishhooks some old
coins and a few ratty
sandal straps
says he

what coins
says willifred
instantly curious

well over there we found
a couple of coins we call
widow s mites
you remember
jesus pointed them out in
mark twelve verses
forty-one to forty-four
a poor widow who put in
two measly mites outgave all
those rich guys because she
gave all she had

what do widow s mites
look like
asks willifred

here s a couple of them
says the hairy goat
they re hardly worth anything
they re the smallest coins in israel

i want them
says willifred
what will you take for them
i ll give you anything i have
just let me have them

and
boss
this greedy gaze
rolled over willifred s eyes
all he could see were those
two little bitty coins

i ve got to have them now
says he
give them to me
give them to me

both the hairy goat and i
backed away very slowly
from willifred
then the hairy goat

Greed Strikes Willifred

lowered his head and said
okay here they come and
the hairy goat then rammed
little willifred and flipped him
heels over head

dazed willifred looked at me
and says
what happened

you re okay now
says me
the greedy bug bit you
and you took a trip to the
funny money farm

boss
it just goes to show
you really have to watch
your motives—we need to
emulate the little
widow s example not
try to amass her assets

amos

The Battling Bug Convention

Of late, Amos has been concerned about the divisions and disunity evident at times in the church pew underworld. However, a recent experience at a large religious gathering of the bug kingdom offered him new hope.

the battling bug convention

boss
we had a convention
the other day
it seemed as if
the whole church pew
underworld was involved
well at least the entire
southern bug section

the mouse media kept
predicting a big bug
showdown—a massive bug
fight—and
boss
when bugs start
to fightin it s guaranteed
to be a nasty mess

the controversy swirled
around the colors and
stripes of the leadership
of the southern bugs
it was the pinstriped
grays versus the
peppermint-striped red-
and-whites and
boss
they ve been
calling each other names—
all sorts of names—but
mostly they ve called
each other un-true bugs
it s enough to drive a
soul buggy
boss

with a certain amount of
tension in the air the
bugs began to select their
top bug for the next year

the mouse media were
eagerly anticipating
whether he would be a
pinstriped gray or a
peppermint-striped
red-and-white

the presiding top bug
sensing the tension in
the air and the danger
of the misguided mouse
media called for a time
of prayer and fasting

prayer virgil the praying
mantis led the way by
organizing prayer clusters
all over the convention
broom closet
the motto of each
prayer cluster was—
every bug to pray every
day come what may

it must ve worked
boss
because when the presiding
top bug gave his top bug
address a holy anointing
filled the convention
broom closet

he preached about healing
hurts in the bug family
he said you heal hurts
in a big bug family just
like you do in any
kind of family

there has to
be a spirit of forgiveness
toward one another
he said
and a spirit of love
one for another and a
spirit of humility in
serving one another

it has to be done
he encouraged each one
there s too much to lose
if we do not choose
to really come together
for the lord can use us
even through this
stormy weather

the presence of the holy
spirit was so strong
boss
that every bug in the place
stood up and bowed
his antennae in repentance
and in humbleness before
the lord and before each other

it was an awesome and
moving experience
boss
after the weeping the joy

and the tears of peace
and harmony there was
hardly a dry bug in the closet

then to climax the events
of the day the presiding
top bug was re elected
and his chief rival was
chosen top bug runner-up
and in the spirit of the
holy spirit s message to
the bug kingdom the two
bugs hugged and a little
bit of the pinstriped gray
rubbed off on the
peppermint-striped red-
and-white and vice versa
not enough to change the
colors and the stripes
exactly but enough to love

boss
maybe a bug hug
would be good for
human bugs too

amos

The Quest for the Holey Cheese, Part One

the quest for the holey cheese

the other day a strange
thing happened
boss
freddie flea and i were
hopping and jogging
around the church kitchen
health-and-fitness trail
when freddie claimed he
heard a rustling sound
behind the stove

you re crazy
says me

no i m not
says he
only ticks and loons
go crazy
besides i know
what i heard
now be a big brave
mouse and go see
what s behind the stove

all right
says me
a bit reluctantly

boss
we tiptoed as only
a mouse and flea can do
up to the stove and peeked
around the corner

there lying on his shell
upside down was an old
mangled turtle with a
tattered piece of paper
hanging limply from his beak

who are you and what
did you do
from where did you come

the old turtle looked at
us with upside-down surprise
i have seen the holey cheese
says he

what cheese
says me
looking around
did you fall
and bust your crown

here flip me over
and i ll tell you a tale
that ll curl your tail
and turn you sober
i have been on
the journey of a lifetime
the greatest search of all
the quest for the holey cheese

what holey cheese
says freddie and me
simultaneously
you re the wackiest
turtle we ve ever seen

no not me
says he
with his feet finally
right-side down
i m the sanest guy around
the smartest one
you ll ever meet
but you re in for a treat
when i tell you of my
daring feat
one sunny day while
floating on my back in
a quiet little pool just
outside the church i saw a
vision of the holey cheese

what holey cheese
freddie and i repeated

the swiss above all swiss
the cheese of plenty
the cheese that ages but
never grows old
the cheese with the perfect
taste but never molds
the cheese that was protected
by joseph of arimathea s cat
and passed down from
century to century from
cat to cat
tis the stuff of dreams
legend and lore
the heart of adventure
thrills and glory galore

last week i found this
crumpled up piece of a
treasure map pointing
the way to the holey cheese

and since you two so
kindly righted myself
why not join old
arthur as his knights
of the round shell
and search the seas
for the holey cheese

and
boss
for such a hot day
in june it sorta seemed
like the right tune to play
and so freddie and me
embarked enthusiastically
on a journey for justice
joy mystery life and peace—
and the holey cheese

amos

p s—next time i ll be home
boss
keep the coffee brewing
the cheese of life sure has a
mysterious flavor away
out here

The Quest for the Holey Cheese, Part Two

Since last week, Amos and Freddie Flea (along with Sammy Salamander), joined Arthur the old mangled turtle on his consuming quest for the holey cheese. Calling themselves the "Knights of Arthur's Round Shell," the foursome marched bravely down the steps of the church basement to encounter whatever adventures awaited them.

the quest for the holey cheese—part two

life is bold
life is great
we re on our way to excavate
the holey cheese from its
resting plate
life is bold
life is great
fraidy cats nor wimps we ain t
we re the toughest in the state
we ll find the cheese
whatever the fate
life is bold
life is great
that s what we have to
celebrate

boss
we were in high spirits
as we marched along
chanting our marching song
but that was before we
knew what dangers lurked
at the bottom of the
basement stairs

first of all
boss
it got darker and darker
the farther we went down
then we started hearing strange
little noises that got louder
as we crawled along

are you sure this
is the way
says i

sure i d know my way
around here if i
was blindfolded
says arthur

methinks he is
blindfolded
whispers freddie to me
and sammy

at the bottom of the stairs
we landed in a heap in a
pile of rags and old clothes
arthur got his head
caught in an oily
shirtsleeve and thought
he got his head stuck
in his shell
help me help me
says he
push on my tail and
wiggle my shell
meanwhile freddie was
buried under an avalanche
of discarded dishtowels
and dirty rags
sammy and i were
holding our own
i felt as though i was
crawling through clothes
tunnels and sammy was sure he

was swimming his way through
a sea of dresses and socks

after pulling freddie free
and showing arthur which
way to go we set off again
but we didn t chant so
loudly this time
boss

in the meantime our
shenanigans disturbed
marcellus the cat and his
alley friends who sometimes
use the clothes pile as their
bed away from home
suddenly we were beset with
a pair of green glowing eyes
about a half a mile up in the
air with other faint glowing
eyes coming at us from the
dark background

run and hide
no time for pride
says i
while darting
for the nearest looming
mop bucket
freddie and sammy jumped
back into the pile of clothes

but arthur was still mad
from his ordeal and started
snapping at everything in—
or out of—sight

ow
yelled marcellus
something bit my foot
let s get out of here
fellas there s a cat trap
down here
and out they went through
the open basement window

and boss while we cheered—
there in the moonlight s glow
rested the holey cheese on
the windowsill beckoning us

after we scrambled over boxes
tools desks bookcases and the
side of the wall to the window
ledge it was gone
exclamation point here
boss
it had disappeared

stunned we headed back to
our homes with no chanting
this time but pondering our
glorious adventure

maybe it wasn t meant to be
boss
because sometimes you
can get so focused on your cause
that you forget to focus on the lord

amos

Joe Cricket and His Buddies

Amos has been reflecting on Independence Day and its relation to spiritual life. He ran across two scriptures—Joshua 24:15, which says, "Choose for yourselves this day whom you will serve.... But as for me and my household, we will serve the Lord." And Galatians 5:1, which says, "For freedom Christ has made us free; Stand fast, therefore, and do not be entangled again with a yoke of bondage."

Using those two passages as a springboard, Amos decided to try his hand at creating a parable.

joe cricket and his buddies

once upon a time
boss
there was a little brown
cricket named joe
joe lived in the lovely
land of crickets grove
a place where all the
crickets sang

joe wanted to be the
best singer in the land
but when he would go to

the clubs he would leave
disgusted and dismayed

most of the clubs were
owned by wicked cricket
the evil prince of crickets
grove and when a cricket sang
for wicked cricket he had to
sing about getting high on
pesticide or the joys of
getting drunk on
sewer water
the other clubs were run by
agents of wicked cricket—
sectsie sal the goddess of
insect lust and rebel rouse
the god of punk bugs

joe wanted to sing praise to
the creator of the land
the lord of crickets grove
and the world beyond

the song of life was in his
heart and legs
boss

since there were no clubs to
sing in joe just began to
sing his song on the
street corners

Joe Cricket and His Buddies

slowly but surely all the
other bugs and crickets began
to come by and listen to his
unusual crooning style
joe s buddies would hop
around and cheer as joe s
popularity grew

however wicked cricket would
send his crowd across the
street to mock jeer and
ridicule him

eventually the cheers were
silenced and joe s buddies
left him and began to go
back to the clubs

joe often saw his buddies
with glazed-over bug eyes
or smelling of soured sewer
water and he would try to
steer them away from
wicked cricket s dens of sin

heck no they would say
we re free to live sing and
play all day

you mean you re free to
waste your life get sick

and die
says joe
you guys can go back to
the clubs where death and
bondage abound but not me
i m set free from
that sort of misery
like you i once was lost
but now i m found
and i sing a new song with
a life-giving sound
all because jesus loves me
and sets me free
that s why i choose to
sing and serve the lord

boss
it s just like joe discovered
there is a freedom that is
real slavery—and a slavery
that is real freedom

amos

p s—who knows maybe one day
we ll all choose god s way
shun the dark
live life as a lark
and enjoy jesus peace joy
and victory

Amos Meets
an Agnostic

amos meets an agnostic

while going through my
college mousebook yesterday
boss
i ran across some
rather haunting memories
staring at me in black and white

to keep from starving to
death through your college
experience
boss
i worked
in the dormitory cafeteria
you remember
it wasn t that bad partly
because of the camaraderie
that developed between me
and harry the golden hamster
harry was a delight
boss
he had a great sense of humor—
he could balance doughnuts
on his nose and keep the

cafeteria crew lighthearted—
he was a model hamster
in fact
boss
he could have passed deacon
inspection in most church pew
underworld congregations

so you can imagine my
surprise one Saturday morning
when i found out he was an
agnostic hamster

how do you get faith
says he
while we were putting out
sweet rolls

what
says me somewhat
incredulously
you mean like in god
says me again
alertness doesn t come easy
for me on saturday mornings
boss

yeah
says he
do you have faith

Amos Meets an Agnostic

uh sure
says me
don t you

no i don t think so
says he

meanwhile
boss
thelma terrapin
a crusty old senior cook
came over and
heard part of the dialogue

you mean you don t believe
in god
she asks

not exactly
says he
i don t know
if i do or not

what do you mean
says me

well i guess i m an agnostic
says he
do you know what an
agnostic is

we shook our heads no

well
says he
i don t think a
person can know for certain
that there is a god
maybe there is
maybe not
now i m not saying there isn t
a god all i m saying is that i
just don t know for sure—
and i don t see how anyone else
can say for sure that there is

all of this did not sit
well with thelma the cook

of course there s a god
says she
who do you think created
the universe

a lot of scientists say that it
evolved over millions of years
and god didn t have anything to
do with it
says he

in genesis it says that god
created the heavens and the

earth—and that s good enough
for me
says she

but how do you know
that for sure
says harry
i would really
like to know if there is a god
or not

silly me
boss
i decided to try
again—harry there is a god and
you can know it for sure

how
says he
how do you know
absolutely for certain that there
is a god when a lot of evidence
would indicate that there may
not be one at all

the main reason we
know god exists
says me
is because the
bible says so

how do you know the bible is
really true
says he

because the bible is god s word
says me

how do you know the bible is
god s word
says he

obviously
boss
the next answer
was going to be because the
bible says so as well as saying
something about its
trustworthiness timelessness
and timeliness

but i could tell that we were
about to be tangled up in a
never-ending cyclical argument
so i decided on a different
approach—after all his questions
had to do with faith

harry
says me
i believe the bible
is true and that it s god s word
because i have faith in him and
in his word that it s so

then how do you get faith
says he

boss
he was asking all
the right questions
i just didn t have the
right answers
for a churchmouse who grew up
in church all his life it was still a
tough question
it had just seemed to me that
faith was always at hand
always available for the asking

it s easy
says me

all you have to do is
believe in jesus—believe
that he died on the cross for
your sins and rose from the
dead so that you can have
everlasting life and full
forgiveness for your sins

how can i believe when i
don t have any faith
says he
you have to have faith to believe
so how do i get faith to believe

boss
it was a real stumper to an
inexperienced witness like me
i was certain that there were
scriptures that applied here—
such as romans ten-eight that
says the word is nigh thee
even in thy mouth and in thy
heart—that is the word of faith—
or romans twelve-three that
says god hath dealt to every
man a measure of faith

but
boss
how could he accept
those passages if he didn t
believe in the bible as god s word

like i said it was a real stumper
and my heart went out to him
i wanted to help and didn t
know how

since then
boss
i ve decided it simply
came down to a matter
of communication
you don t communicate faith
intellectually
intellectual arguments run out
eventually and frustration
often sets in
but that can be good
boss
because it can lead a person
to the real point of faith

faith isn t an intellectual process
it s a heart matter
an exercise—not of the mind—
but of the will
faith without action is dead
faith in the mind is stillborn
but faith in the heart moves
mountains—and saves souls

amos

A Cloudy Vision

a cloudy vision

boss
i don t know
if you ve ever talked
to a cloud
but i did
the other day
it was a misty experience

i was strolling
through the dandelions
in the church yard
just minding my
own business when
this little cloud
descends on me
from out of the
sky and surrounds
me with fog and
water droplets

without thinking
i shouted out
hey whatcha doing

you re blocking my sun
and ruining my fun
go away
okay

no
said he
and his voice was
just a little rumble
i need someone
to storm at
and build
a little thunder

but why
said i

some clouds are
made for rain
some for storms
hail and wind
i m the stormy sort
he sang
i blast rumble
and bend
i shout flash
and raise cain
and people run
when they see me come
i chuckle and snort
it s a real good sport

in fact
he whispered thunderously
people name their troubles
after me
the stormy trials of life
they say
and they fret when i
come out to play

but what about
i tried to shout
the silver lining
roundabout
to help us out
and stop our pining

oh that old riff
he sniffed
it s just a myth

just then
boss
a great gargantuan
fluffy cloud floated
lightly over us all
so stunningly awesome
was he that he
glowed from the
inside out and
i nearly twice
passed out

this little puff
he huffed
don t know his stuff
he s so impressed
with his own little bell
and how much he himself
has to tell
that he doesn t recognize
the dong on a gong
nor even the song

we clouds
he continued to say
have a purpose
both night and day
we bring
shade and rain
rest and life
he sang
but much
more than that—
and here s where
it s at—
we resonate in
reality the power
of jesus victory
and demonstrate
in majesty
the presence of his glory

that s right
said i

A Cloudy Vision

if we look up high
we ll see him
in our skies

so with that
said and done
both clouds rose
and boss i saw
the sun—and my toes

says the apostle john
in revelation one
behold he cometh
with clouds
and no matter
how stormy or loud
his presence within them
can be found

boss
the clouds in my life
may bring
storms and strife
tears and rain
but he comes with
clouds to set us free
and within those clouds
we all can see
him in his power glory
and victory

amos

The High-falutin' Frog

the high-falutin frog

boss
you remember jonah
the high-falutin frog
the fellow who always
thought he was better
than everybody else—
especially toads and
mice and all other
varieties of god s creatures

now they call him
jonah the gourdhead

why
you ask
i ll tell you why
actually it s a rather
simple task as a matter
of fact

you see
boss
the lord

told jonah the frog
to hop to the eastern
sky to the land of
the toads

but poor jonah couldn t
stand toads
boss
in fact he used to say
that toads were dumber
than clay—and clay was
dumber than amalgamated
dirt—but he said at least
clay was more useful
than toads were

still the lord told him
to go east to preach to
those toads
so what did jonah the
high-falutin frog do
he joyfully hopped west
as fast as his fat little
legs could spring

but then while he was
crossing the wild western desert
a rip-roaring sandstorm
slashed across the dunes

The High-falutin' Frog

while trying to hop and
hide behind a big black
boulder jonah suddenly
found that boulder had
turned into the cavernous
mouth of pecos pete
the legendary boa
constrictor

and before you knew
it boss ol jonah the
high-falutin frog was
swallowed whole

well it didn t take jonah
long before he started
hopping around in that
viper s belly
hollering for the lord
first to forgive him
then second to save him

sure enough after a few
miles across those
blazing desert dunes
pecos pete got the
awfullest stomachache
boss
and out came ol
slippery slimy jonah
headed lickety-split
east to the land of
the toads

and
boss
as soon as he
arrived in toadville he
started preaching doom
death and destruction
to all toads
you could tell he was
going to be a real
popular guy there
boss

The High-falutin' Frog

but it worked
those toads repented
from the top of their
little pointy heads to
their flat webbed feet

was jonah happy boss—
not at all
in fact he wished
he had never been born
and then he hopped
over to a nearby lily
pad to sulk

the lord then grew
a plant complete with
a little gourd to protect
him from the hot sun
the blowing dust and the
dismal storms

the next day
though
the lord let the plant
and gourd die
and jonah the high-
falutin frog also wanted
to die

what s the matter with you
the lord said

are you angry because
of the gourd

yes sir
jonah said
i liked the little gourd

see how you are
the lord said
here you are
caring about a gourd
when there are so many
toads who need me and
you—jonah
you re a real gourdhead
the lord chided him

and
boss
that s how jonah
the high-falutin frog
became a gourdhead—
by caring more about
things than other folks

amos

Amos Finds
a Harmonica

amos finds a harmonica

boss
i was strolling out
behind the music store next
to the church building the
other day and i stumbled
across this metal object
with square holes on the side

what s this
says me
to freddy the flea
who happened to be hopping
alongside of me

beats me
says he
maybe it s a
bus turned topsy-turvy

yeah or maybe it s a round house
that s lost its swervy
says bertie woeworm
just wiggling by

what are we talking about
and why
says the doom-and-gloom guy

this strange metal-and-wood
contraption
says me
exasperatedly

maybe it s an apartment
building for aphids
says sammy salamander
who floated nearby

it s a harmonica
says wise old oliver owl
didn t you creatures
ever study music and art
appreciation

all i studied was feline detestation
says me

and all i learned was boredom
sourdom and pessimism
says bertie

and i learned to play on
all the world s great waterways
says sammy

Amos Finds a Harmonica

so how do you play
this musical thing
says me

you huff and puff and puff
and huff until you make
musical notes and stuff
says oliver owl

it sounds like it was made
for big bad wolves and not
for little gray mice
says me

try it
amos
make it sing
says freddy and sammy
with a harmonious ring

so boss i huffed and i puffed
and i puffed and i huffed
but to no avail
the harmonica silently
snickered at me with
snaggled teeth
till i turned pale
but boss i took a
deep breath and blew with
all my mousey might
and a sound came out

i nearly passed out from fright
all my friends ran for cover
and then wanted to know
when it was over

but i began to learn how
to play by breathing out
and breathing in
i couldn t make
the blues sound but i
could make my voice quiver

inside the harmonica box
cover i found the
instructions and how to
play such favorites as
kum bah yah and when
the saints go marchin in
i learned to play kum
bah yah but only part
of the saints song

after a couple of weeks
of kum ba yah over and
over again
the music critics crept
out of the woods
boss

Amos Finds a Harmonica

don t you know any hymns
says the leader of the
ladybug choir

you need to learn some
contemporary songs
says willifred the white rat

what about some good ol
country music or rock n roll
says manfred the millipede

stop playing those goofy
choruses and learn some
classic dignified hymns
cried clara centipede
stamping all thirty-two
of her little feet

boss
i had to drag myself and
my harmonica to safety
and i began to practice in
the catacombs underneath
the church pew underworld

you see all i wanted to do
was to learn some music
to praise and worship jesus

amos

Amos Converses with a Bone

amos converses with a bone

willifred the white rat talked
me into taking another trip
in his tiny time traveler
the other day
boss

let s go visit ezekiel in the
valley of the dry bones
says willifred
and he set the time
traveler to about
five hundred eighty b c

after a few whooshes and
whirring sounds the time
traveler stopped
willifred and i stepped outside
and nearly fainted at the sight

a valley spread out before us
but it wasn t empty boss—it
was full of dead dry bones
bones scattered here and

there and everywhere
just like the scene described
in ezekiel chapter thirty-seven
boss

so whatchu gawking at
a voice came
from the valley floor
it had an eerie quality
like a creaking door

whaddayu mean
says me timidly
where are you
come out and show me
where you be

here i am
right before your nose
take two more steps
and i ll trip up your toes
now go away
and leave me alone
nobody here cares a whit
about an old dry bone

boss
it was a bit spooky
talking to a bone in a
god-forsaken valley but
finally i asked

what happened to you
this looks worse than
napoleon s waterloo

aw who cares
says the bone indifferently
nobody cares whether we live
or die or flee or fly
so go away
go play
in a pile of hay
i don t care
just don t stay

that sure is a grumpy
old bone
says willifred to me
i agree
says me

yeah well you d be grumpy
too if you couldn t
find your shoe—
or even your left hand—
says the bone
lying in the sand
besides i hate little furry rodents
who act like people
so go away
go jump off a steeple

so willifred and i turned to
leave when just then this
hairy-looking prophet guy
gets beamed down nearly
on top of me

then a voice boomed out
of the sky
ezekiel son of man
prophesy to those bones
tell them they ll come alive
they ll take on flesh
and skin and survive

big deal
says the bone
what difference will that make
we ll still be dead
inside we may look alive
but our souls are fried
we may be able to stand
but we re still just an
upright piece of sand

and boss he was right but
after ezekiel prophesied
all those bones shook and
rattled and came together
bone to bone and joint to
joint complete with tendons
flesh and blood

quite a change from
bleached bone and dusty sod

again
the lord boomed
from heaven to the hairy prophet
prophesy for the spirit to blow from
the four winds to fill these
bones and men

and
boss
that s what happened
the spirit blew across that
valley and those bones-turned-men
became a mighty living army
for the lord

i ll place my spirit in you
and you shall live
i ll open your graves
and give you back your
life and land

then the bone who was now
a mighty man said
wow what a god
what a great plan—
and boss he had a grin
as wide as an ocean span

it just goes to show you
boss
life takes on a new perspective
when god s spirit touches you

amos

The Nightmare Trauma

the nightmare trauma

boss
you should never eat
day-old pizza slices leftover
from a church youth party
it creates strange visions—
and not those of the biblical sort

last night i went to sleep
in my little matchbox bed
and immediately dreamed
of falling into a dark deep
hole in the earth
the fall was punctuated
by bursts of fireworks
that transformed
into snarling alley cat faces

suddenly there was a big
flash of light and i found
myself trying to wade
through a melted chocolate
bar to get to a dangling
piece of gourmet swiss

cheese held just beyond
me by green aliens from roswell

indiana jones never had it
this bad
says me
still trudging
through chocolate that was
rapidly turning into molasses

deciding that no cheese
was worth that kind of struggle
i suddenly found myself at the
end of no mouse land being
chased by a really angry
runaway ferris wheel

at the edge of the cliff where
no mouse land ends there was
a circus ringmaster who kept
handing out tickets and saying
go directly to the circus
do not pass go
do not collect two hundred dollars
and do not feed
the elephants or the mice

immediately
boss
a big gray
elephant swung through the

The Nightmare Trauma

trees on a grapevine to
rescue me and take me to
a for-he s-a jolly-good-mouse
party sponsored by alley
cats for a better society

the cats kept trying to kill
me with kindness
boss
they tried to feed me a
big bite of cake but i kept
refusing it because i knew
that it would blow me up
and i would eventually be
served as happy birthday
mouse pate to the world s
feline population

no no no
they would purr
with their whiskered grins
we want to be your friend
we want to play games with
you and love you to the
very end

for some reason
boss
i didn t believe them
then it occurred
to me that i was just like

peter on the rooftop in acts
having visions of clean and
unclean animals

i was just on the verge of
deciding to take a bite of the
cake when freddie the flea
landed right in the middle of
my tummy and kept hopping
up and down

wake up wake up amos he was
yelling and bouncing up and
down

why what s the matter
says i

well besides your snoring
you re yelling and screaming
and tossing and turning and
you re keeping the whole
church pew underworld awake
and miserable

visions and dreams
are one thing
boss and can often
come from the lord
but nightmares
are something else

like i said
don t ever
eat day-old pizza leftover
from a church youth party

amos

Bertie Gets Revived, Part One

bertie gets revived—part one

boss
i saw bertie woeworm
the other day
not deliberately
no one deliberately goes to
see bertie woeworm
he s the sort of fellow who
when he walks into a
room you feel like
somebody just turned
out the lights

bertie was crying
it s so sad
he said
the world is worse
than really bad

bugs on drugs
wars and pesticides
attacks on ladybugs
crime and sewer-cide

it s enough
he cried
to make a toad
run and hide

what with owlless night
and rainy days
trapdoor spiders and
the skunk-sprayed haze
the mouse media
biased in favor of mice
the ants get drunk
and dance
the roaches have all
turned to nightly poaches
and mosquitoes dive bomb
diseases on all their foes-es

Bertie Gets Revived, Part One

it s enough
he cried
to make a dog
run and hide

but he wept and wailed
as if he d been jailed
as bad as all this
worldly strife
nothing s so sad as
the state of my life

my life s been
so boring and dull
it s been one
unbroken lull

i m the epitome
of mediocrity

being with me
he sighed
is about as fun and high
as watching paint dry

the kids laugh and joke
fun at me they poke
what s lower than an
pet rock s i q they say
bertie woeworm they cry
and run off to play

oh it s enough
he cried
to make a monkey
run and hide

my life has no real
meaning or purpose
i m good only to be
fed to a porpoise

it would seem my life s
only goal is met at
the end of the road
with nothing
much in between
save a small groan
and a scream

mediocre in birth
mediocre in death

imagine—no eulogy no
last wish—just sorta
swallowed whole by a
large fish

i tell you
he told me
i m the epitome of
mediocrity

even my mediocrity
is mediocre
don t you see

oh it s enough
he cried
to make a donkey
run and hide

boss
they tell me
that the first step
toward revival is
a long hard look at
yourself and an
honest confession of
your shortcomings

but methinks that ole
bertie s being a little
too tough on himself

i m not sure whether
even god can pull him
out of his pit of despair

amos

Bertie Gets Revived, Part Two

Last week, Amos bumped into Bertie Woeworm, who was bemoaning the "sad state" of his life.

bertie gets revived—part two

i tell you
he told me
i m the epitome
of mediocrity

but just then
boss
rawley eagle came flying by
except he was
about two miles high

bertie
i cried
an eagle i ve spied
oh help
he cried
there s nowhere to hide
he ll eat me
he ll eat me
he sighed

even the fish
will be denied
oh mediocre me
scooped up to eternity

by now
boss
rawley had landed
and bertie was belly-up
with his eyes closed

rawley asked why so grim
what s the matter with him

he thinks he s about
to die
says i

but how can that be
since it s only me
says he

he thinks you re out
to chomp on him and that
his life is empty and slim

oh not so little bro—
i came to teach
you to fly
a way up high
in that sky

but woeworms can t
fly in skies
says i

oh they can fly
if they learn how to die

bertie rolled over
right side up
wait a minute
there buttercup
how can a
woeworm fly
after he s had to die
i think it s a big lie

oh no go-slow
rawley said
and shook his head
you don t
understand the plan man
you can be free
from the land stan
you can be a butterfly
if you ll surrender and die

sure just jump in your beak
and lie there nice and meek

no no you make
a pretty cocoon
while you whistle
a sad-happy tune
and then in a deep
sleep you will swoon
to come out a flier
at high noon

you mean you won t
eat me
asked bertie

no not me
says rawley
don t you see
i came to you
out of the blue

Bertie Gets Revived, Part Two

to so love you
that you
won t be afraid to die
but will start
to mount up on high
with the wings of a butterfly

you can live free
says he
if you ll turn from
your me
and trust jesus victory

just die to self and sin
let jesus burst on in
woeworm butterflies can win
and worms and eagles
can be friends

and
boss
rawley gave
bertie the biggest hug
that slug ever had

and bertie actually
grinned
exclamation point

i have decided
boss

that many a woeworm
among us could be
revived with a bit of
jesus love and a hug

amos

Printed in the United States
R4316400001B/R43164PG125692LVX1B/1/P9